Ridiculous Things People Actually Believe

A Field Guide to Spectacular Intellectual Failure

Richard Lowe

The Writing King

Table of Contents

See books by Richard Lowe at
https://masterofworlds.com

Get free publishing insights and industry updates at
https://thewritingking.substack.com

For ghostwriting and book coaching services see
https://thewritingking.com

Introduction

I didn't set out to write a book about stupidity. I set out to figure out why people I respect — smart people, curious people, people who can operate spreadsheets and parallel park — have started believing things that would have landed them in a padded room fifty years ago.

Forty-five years in technology taught me one thing above everything else: there is a hard difference between things that work and things people want to work. A database either stores the data or it doesn't. A network either routes the packets or it doesn't. You don't get to believe your way to a different outcome. Reality has opinions, and they are not negotiable.

So watching people drink bleach to cure cancer while refusing chemotherapy, watching parents leave children vulnerable to diseases we eradicated decades ago, watching grown adults spend real money on psychics and crystals and manifestation coaches — it doesn't just baffle me. It makes me angry. These are not harmless hobbies. Some of them kill people. Some of them kill children.

This book is not a compassionate exploration of why misinformation happens. There are plenty of those, and they are very polite, and they have not fixed anything. This is a direct examination of specific beliefs, why they are wrong, and how people manage to hold them while surrounded by evidence of their wrongness. I am not interested in validating the journey. I am interested in the destination, which is usually embarrassing and occasionally catastrophic.

Each chapter covers a different category of belief: the flat earthers, the medical quacks, the celebrity death hoaxers, the secret society watchers, the space conspiracy crowd, and more. Each one follows the same structure: here is what they believe, here is where it came from, here is why it is wrong, and here is my honest reaction to the whole thing. You will notice the honest reaction is rarely charitable. That is intentional.

The last few chapters step back from the specific beliefs and look at the machinery underneath: the logical fallacies, the cognitive biases, the social media dynamics that turn individual delusion into organized movements. If you read the whole book, you will end up with a fairly complete picture of how ordinary human brains get weaponized against their owners.

One more thing before we start. I am not presenting myself as someone immune to any of this. I have owned a lucky shirt. I have knocked on wood. The difference between me and the people in this book is not that I am incapable of irrational thinking — it is that I have never let irrational thinking kill anyone. That bar, depressingly, turns out to be higher than you would expect.

Let's get into it.

Chapter 1: Flat Earth and Hollow Earth

Chapter Introduction

Welcome to our grand tour of people who used their textbooks as coasters and their science classes as naptime. This chapter explores humans in 2026 who can order pizza with their phones, livestream their breakfast to strangers, and navigate using satellites they claim don't exist, yet have convinced themselves that our planet looks like a dinner plate or contains underground civilizations with better Wi-Fi than most apartment complexes.

We're diving into three spectacular examples of weaponized stupidity: the modern flat earth movement (for people who think thousands of years of astronomy was elaborate performance art), hollow earth beliefs (our planet is a geological Kinder Egg), and ice wall conspiracies (Antarctica is Earth's cosmic pool fence, installed by celestial HOA officials).

These people perform Olympic-level mental gymnastics while using GPS to drive to conferences where they explain why GPS is a lie. They argue that water doesn't curve while booking round-trip flights on routes that only work because Earth is round. Picture someone insisting rain isn't wet while getting soaked in a thunderstorm.

The psychology involves confirmation bias, motivated reasoning, and the intellectual equivalent of sticking your fingers in your ears and shouting "LA LA LA I CAN'T HEAR YOU" at physics. Strap in. We're about to watch thousands of people convince themselves that basic geography is the world's most elaborate practical joke.

What They Believe

Modern flat earthers claim our planet is a flat disc with the North Pole at the center and Antarctica forming an ice wall around the perimeter, like the world's worst lazy Susan. The sun and moon are small, local objects (pizza-sized) circling above this disc like the universe's most disappointing mobile.

They believe gravity doesn't exist because the invisible force keeping your coffee in your mug is too mainstream. Instead, the flat Earth disc accelerates upward at 9.8 meters per second squared, explaining why things fall down. They think our entire planet is a cosmic elevator accelerating upward for billions of years without reaching its destination.

The most prominent voices: Mark Sargent, Patricia Steere, and Daniel Shenton, who spread these ideas through YouTube videos and conferences with the evangelical fervor of people selling extended warranties for toasters.

They claim NASA, world governments, and scientists engage in a massive conspiracy to hide the "truth" about Earth's shape, though they're vague about why anyone would bother. Nothing says "efficient conspiracy" like requiring every airline pilot, ship captain, and physics teacher to keep the same secret for generations without spilling the beans on TikTok.

Origins and History

The modern movement traces back to Samuel Birley Rowbotham (1816-1884), who peaked during his "questioning everything" phase and never moved on. He published "Zetetic Astronomy" in 1849 under the pseudonym "Parallax." Nothing says "I'm definitely not crazy" like using a fake name to publish revolutionary geographic theories.

Rowbotham based his ideas on his 1838 Bedford Level experiment, where he stood by a canal, squinted at some boats, and concluded Earth must be flat because he couldn't see curvature. This is like looking at your kitchen table and concluding all furniture is rectangular.

The movement gained momentum in the 2010s through YouTube personalities like Mark Sargent, who discovered flat earth theory online and thought, "This seems legit." The internet is known for reliable geographic information, after all.

Why It's Asinine

The flat earth model can't explain seasons, time zones, or why different constellations are visible from different latitudes. If the sun were a local spotlight doing donuts above a flat disc, people in Australia and Canada would see the same stars, and everyone would experience seasons simultaneously.

The logistics of maintaining such a conspiracy would require every airline pilot, ship captain, GPS satellite operator, astronaut, government official, physicist, and geography teacher to be in on it. That's millions of people keeping the same secret for decades without a credible whistleblower. Meanwhile, these same people can't keep celebrity divorces secret for five minutes.

Flat earthers can't even agree on their own model. Some claim Earth accelerates upward to explain gravity, others reject gravity entirely. Some say the ice wall is guarded by NASA agents with penguin battalions, others think there are multiple ice walls.

The December 2024 "Final Experiment" expedition took flat earthers to Antarctica, where they witnessed the 24-hour sun (impossible on their model). Even prominent believers had to admit their model was wrong. The community's response? They declared the expedition fake and accused their own believers of being government agents.

My Commentary

I'm not sure what's more baffling: that people believe this nonsense or that they're so confident they'll argue with rocket scientists while using devices proving them wrong. We can watch live streams from space, track satellites with phone apps, and send up weather balloons to see Earth's curvature. Yet thousands have convinced themselves that their inability to see curvature from the Walmart parking lot trumps centuries of scientific observation.

The flat earth movement is what happens when someone mistakes being contrarian for being intelligent. Real critical thinking involves examining evidence, not reflexively rejecting anything challenging your preconceptions while yelling "FAKE NEWS!" at physics textbooks.

Here's the kicker: flat earthers use GPS devices (working because Earth is spherical) to navigate to conferences where they explain why GPS is a government conspiracy. They book flights following great circle routes (only making sense on a sphere) to attend meetings where they discuss why sphere Earth is impossible. Think of someone using a ladder to climb up and give a speech about how ladders don't exist.

What They Believe

Hollow earth proponents claim our planet contains vast hollow spaces with underground civilizations having better urban planning than most surface cities. The popular version suggests Earth has a hollow interior accessible through large openings at the poles, often called "Symmes Holes."

More elaborate versions propose multiple concentric spheres within Earth, each harboring ecosystems and inhabitants, like Russian nesting dolls designed by someone who failed geology. Some blend hollow earth with UFO theories, suggesting flying saucers come from inner space, not outer space. Even aliens prefer basement apartments.

Origins and History

The theory has a distinguished scientific pedigree, making its modern persistence embarrassing. English astronomer Edmond Halley proposed it in 1692. Other brilliant mathematicians like Leonhard Euler got involved, because even geniuses can have wrong ideas about where we live.

The real star was John Cleves Symmes Jr. (1780-1829), who spent his life trying to secure funding for polar expeditions to find these openings, like a persistent salesman trying to sell people on secret planetary entrances.

Why It's Asinine

We have extensive seismic data from earthquakes showing Earth's internal structure: thin crust, thick mantle of hot rock, core of iron and nickel. Seismic waves travel at predictable speeds based on materials they encounter. If Earth were hollow, these waves would behave completely differently.

We'd have detected hollow Earth through gravitational measurements. A hollow Earth would have less mass and less gravitational pull. Your bathroom scale would give different readings and NASA would have recalculated every satellite orbit. Our gravity measurements match perfectly with a solid planet.

Modern satellite imagery shows no giant holes at the poles. GPS systems work precisely because they calculate positions based on a solid, spherical Earth. If there were continent-sized holes, every GPS device would be useless.

My Commentary

Hollow earth theory is charmingly delusional, like a geological fairy tale. There's something optimistic about imagining underground civilizations with good drilling technology to avoid poking through to our side.

But we literally have X-ray vision for the planet using seismic waves. We can peer into Earth's interior with the precision doctors use to examine broken bones. Yet believers act like the planet's interior is an unknowable mystery, like they're living in the 18th century when the most advanced earth-scanning technology was a big shovel.

If there were massive polar openings, wouldn't airlines have noticed? Do they think pilots are terrible at their jobs, or that everyone who's flown over the Arctic is part of a conspiracy of geographical incompetence?

What They Believe

Ice wall conspiracy theorists claim Antarctica isn't a continent but a massive ice wall surrounding the edges of flat Earth, like the universe's most expensive pool fence. This wall prevents oceans from flowing off the edge and hides whatever lies beyond.

They claim the 1959 Antarctic Treaty prevents people from discovering this ice wall. NASA and world governments patrol this barrier with elite ice guards whose job includes "preventing tourists from discovering our planet is dinner plate-shaped."

Origins and History

The concept springs from Samuel Rowbotham's 1849 flat earth model. This predates Antarctic exploration, making it like writing a restaurant review for a place you've never visited.

Captain James Clark Ross encountered Antarctic ice barriers in 1839-1843, discovering "The Great Barrier" with 100-meter cliffs. This dramatic encounter provided fuel for flat earth theorists, who interpreted natural ice shelves as boundary walls.

Why It's Asinine

Antarctica is not a wall. It's a continent. A big, cold, thoroughly mapped continent with interior regions, mountains, research stations, and all the features of a landmass existing in three dimensions. We have detailed satellite imagery and thousands of researchers who've worked there.

The Antarctic Treaty doesn't prevent civilian visits. Thousands of tourists visit annually through organized expeditions, posting Instagram photos. You can Google "Antarctic cruises" and book a trip right now.

The December 2024 "Final Experiment" took flat earthers to Antarctica, where they witnessed the 24-hour sun (impossible on flat Earth). The community rejected the results and accused their own members of conspiracy.

My Commentary

The ice wall conspiracy might be the most easily debunked belief in this book. We're talking about the basic shape of a continent thousands have visited and photographed.

Believers claim the Antarctic Treaty prevents access while being oblivious that you can book Antarctic cruises online like ordering pizza. Either this conspiracy is run by the most incompetent secret organization in history, or Antarctica is exactly what scientists say: a cold continent at the bottom of our spherical planet.

These believers carry GPS devices working because Earth is spherical while believing satellites are fake. They use the evidence against their beliefs to navigate to meetings where they discuss how that evidence doesn't exist. It's like someone insisting fire can't exist while using a lighter to read the pamphlet explaining why fire can't exist.

Chapter 2: Medical Miracles and Dangerous Delusions

Chapter Introduction

Welcome to the magical world of people who think their immune system needs a software update, water has better memory than they do, and drinking their own urine is a health strategy instead of a cry for help. This chapter explores humans who will spend $200 on crystal healing sessions while claiming they can't afford medical care, and folks who believe Big Pharma is out to get them while trusting random Facebook posts about miracle cures written by someone whose biggest medical qualification is owning a WebMD bookmark.

We're diving into seven spectacular examples of desperate hope meeting aggressive stupidity: the anti-vaccine movement (leaving children defenseless against diseases we already defeated), vaccines-cause-autism believers (the fraudulent study that refuses to die), vaccine microchip theorists (for people who think Bill Gates wants to track their trips to Walmart), homeopathy (where less medicine somehow equals more healing), crystal healing and energy medicine (rocks are better doctors than doctors), bleach as a miracle cure (cleaning products doubling as medicine), and urine therapy (drinking your own waste products is somehow healthier than drinking water).

These beliefs aren't just detached from basic biology and chemistry. They require breathtaking arrogance to dismiss centuries of medical research while trusting YouTube videos made by people who think "doing your own research" means reading memes in Facebook groups.

These folks reject proven treatments saving millions of lives but enthusiastically embrace "natural" remedies that would make medieval plague doctors roll their eyes.

The psychology involves magical thinking, the naturalistic fallacy, and the intellectual equivalent of playing Russian roulette with your health. Let's get into it.

What They Believe

Anti-vaccine activists claim vaccines are dangerous, unnecessary, and cause more harm than the diseases they prevent. They argue natural immunity is superior to vaccine-induced immunity, that childhood diseases like measles and polio are harmless "rites of passage," and that the human immune system is perfectly capable of handling any infection without medical intervention. According to this worldview, vaccines are a conspiracy by pharmaceutical companies to create lifelong customers by deliberately weakening immune systems and causing chronic diseases.

Modern anti-vaxxers promote vaccines containing dangerous toxins, heavy metals, and foreign DNA poisoning children and causing everything from autism to ADHD to sudden infant death syndrome. They claim vaccine injury is vastly underreported, that doctors are either ignorant or complicit in covering up vaccine dangers, and that parents who vaccinate their children are poisoning them on behalf of Big Pharma.

The movement has evolved from religious and philosophical objections to vaccines into a sophisticated misinformation network spreading through social media, alternative health websites, and celebrity endorsements. Anti-vaxxers present themselves as brave truth-tellers fighting against medical tyranny, often comparing vaccination requirements to Nazi Germany or communist oppression.

Some believers extend their opposition to all modern medicine, promoting alternative treatments like homeopathy, chiropractic care, and dietary supplements as superior alternatives to conventional medical care. They often overlap with other conspiracy theories, viewing vaccines as part of larger plots involving population control, government surveillance, or global elite manipulation.

Why It's Asinine

Vaccines are among the greatest public health achievements in human history. They've eliminated smallpox globally, nearly eradicated polio, and prevented millions of deaths from diseases once killing or disabling countless children. The diseases vaccines prevent aren't harmless childhood experiences. They're serious illnesses causing permanent disability, brain damage, and death.

The supposed "toxins" in vaccines exist in quantities so small they're medically insignificant. Formaldehyde, often cited as a dangerous vaccine ingredient, is produced naturally by the human body in quantities far exceeding what's found in vaccines. The aluminum in vaccines is less than what infants consume in breast milk or formula. These people are more worried about trace amounts of preservatives in vaccines than actual deadly diseases.

The "natural immunity is better" argument ignores acquiring natural immunity requires surviving the disease first, which isn't guaranteed. Measles kills about 1 in 1,000 infected children and causes permanent complications in many more. Polio paralyzed thousands of children annually before vaccines. Natural immunity from smallpox required surviving one of history's most deadly diseases. Vaccines provide immunity without the risks of the disease.

The vaccine injury claims are wildly exaggerated. The Vaccine Adverse Event Reporting System (VAERS), often cited by anti-vaxxers, is a passive surveillance system where anyone can report anything happening after vaccination, regardless of whether vaccines caused it. Anti-vaxxers treat VAERS reports as proven causation when they're simply temporal correlation. It's like blaming vaccines for car accidents happening the day after vaccination.

Countries with high vaccination rates have lower rates of childhood mortality and infectious disease than countries with low vaccination rates. Areas where vaccination rates drop due to anti-vaccine activism consistently see outbreaks of preventable diseases. The 2019 measles outbreak in the Pacific Northwest, driven by low vaccination rates, infected dozens of children and cost millions in public health response.

My Commentary

The anti-vaccine movement represents the triumph of fear over evidence and emotion over logic. These people have convinced themselves they're protecting their children by leaving them vulnerable to deadly diseases vaccines prevent. It's like refusing to use car seats because you read somewhere that seat belts can cause injuries, while ignoring that car accidents kill children regularly.

The scientific illiteracy here is breathtaking. Anti-vaxxers will spend hours researching vaccine ingredients on conspiracy websites but won't bother learning basic immunology or understanding how clinical trials work. They'll trust the opinion of a former Playboy model or a disgraced British doctor over the collective knowledge of every major medical organization in the world.

The selfishness is equally stunning. Anti-vaxxers rely on other people vaccinating their children to maintain herd immunity while refusing to contribute to that protection themselves. They're free-riding on everyone else's responsible choices while claiming moral superiority for endangering their own kids and others.

The body count is real. Children die because of anti-vaccine beliefs. When parents choose fear over science, their children pay the price. We've seen preventable deaths from influenza, whooping cough, and other vaccine-preventable diseases in unvaccinated children whose parents thought they knew better than centuries of medical research.

Anti-vaxxers often claim to be following their "maternal instincts" or "doing research" while ignoring the most basic parental responsibility: protecting their children from preventable harm. They've been convinced that protecting their kids means leaving them defenseless against diseases killing millions throughout history.

Vaccines Cause Autism

What They Believe

Despite being thoroughly debunked by numerous large-scale studies, many people still believe vaccines cause autism spectrum disorders. This belief stems primarily from a fraudulent 1998 study by British doctor Andrew Wakefield, who claimed to have found a link between the MMR (measles, mumps, rubella) vaccine and autism. Believers argue that the timing of autism diagnoses coinciding with childhood vaccination schedules proves causation, and that increasing autism rates parallel expanding vaccine schedules.

Proponents claim vaccines overwhelm young immune systems, that multiple vaccines given simultaneously cause brain inflammation leading to autism, and that vaccine ingredients like thimerosal (a mercury-containing preservative) cause neurological damage. They point to parents' anecdotal reports of children regressing after vaccination and argue that the medical establishment covers up vaccine injuries to protect pharmaceutical profits.

The belief has expanded beyond the original MMR vaccine to include claims that any vaccine can trigger autism, that children receive "too many, too soon," and that spreading out or delaying vaccines reduces autism risk. Some believers promote alternative vaccination schedules, while others reject all vaccines entirely, preferring to risk serious diseases instead of facing the imagined autism risk.

Modern vaccine-autism believers often incorporate other conspiracy theories, claiming autism is a form of vaccine injury being deliberately hidden by corrupt doctors, government agencies, and pharmaceutical companies. They promote unproven treatments for "vaccine-injured" autistic children: dangerous chelation therapy, hyperbaric oxygen, and various supplements.

Why It's Asinine

The original study linking vaccines to autism was retracted by The Lancet medical journal after investigators found Wakefield had falsified data, failed to disclose financial conflicts of interest, and conducted unethical experiments on children. Wakefield lost his medical license and was banned from practicing medicine in the UK. The study was not just wrong. It was fraudulent from the beginning.

Multiple large-scale studies involving millions of children have found no link between vaccines and autism. A 2019 Danish study following over 650,000 children found no association between MMR vaccination and autism, even among children with autism risk factors. Studies examining thimerosal, vaccination timing, and total vaccine exposure have all reached the same conclusion: vaccines don't cause autism.

The timing argument is a classic example of confusing correlation with causation. Autism symptoms typically become apparent around 18-24 months of age, coinciding with the standard childhood vaccination schedule. This temporal relationship doesn't prove causation any more than most children learning to walk around the same time proves vaccines cause walking.

Autism rates have continued to increase even after thimerosal was removed from most childhood vaccines in 2001. If mercury in vaccines caused autism, removing it should have led to decreasing autism rates. Instead, rates continued to rise, suggesting other factors (improved recognition, broader diagnostic criteria, better access to services) explain the increases.

The biological mechanisms proposed by vaccine-autism believers don't make scientific sense. Autism is a neurodevelopmental condition with strong genetic components beginning before birth. Brain differences associated with autism are present in prenatal brain development, long before any vaccines are administered. That vaccines could retroactively cause developmental changes occurring in the womb defies basic biology.

Countries with different vaccination schedules and different autism diagnostic criteria show similar autism prevalence rates, contradicting claims that specific vaccine practices cause autism. Unvaccinated children develop autism at the same rates as vaccinated children, which should be impossible if vaccines were the cause.

My Commentary

The vaccine-autism belief might be the most destructive medical myth of the modern era, because it combines legitimate parental concern with scientific fraud to create a fear literally killing children. Parents desperately seeking explanations for their child's autism diagnosis were given a false villain by a con man who manipulated their love and concern for personal profit.

The persistence of this belief after overwhelming scientific evidence debunking it shows how powerful confirmation bias can be when combined with parental desperation. These parents want someone or something to blame for their child's condition, and vaccines provide a convenient target feeling more controllable than genetic lottery or random developmental variation.

The tragedy is compounded by avoiding vaccines not preventing autism but leaving children vulnerable to potentially deadly diseases. These parents think they're protecting their children from autism by skipping vaccines, but they're trading an imaginary risk for very real ones while their children remain just as likely to be autistic.

The autism community has repeatedly stated this belief is harmful because it implies autism is a fate worse than death from preventable diseases, and that autistic children are damaged goods needing to be "recovered" from their condition. This stigmatizes autism and leads to harmful "treatments" seriously injuring autistic children.

The original fraud is still running. It continues to cause harm more than two decades later. Andrew Wakefield's lies have killed more children than his medical career ever saved, yet he continues to profit from spreading anti-vaccine misinformation while hiding behind the pain of parents he helped mislead. It's a perfect example of how one person's greed and dishonesty can create suffering echoing through generations.

The vaccine-autism myth represents everything wrong with how misinformation spreads in the internet age: emotional appeal trumping evidence, anecdotes overwhelming data, and fear defeating hope. Until we learn to value scientific evidence over viral videos, children will continue to pay the price for adult ignorance.

What They Believe

Modern anti-vaccine conspiracy theorists claim COVID-19 vaccines (and increasingly, all vaccines) contain microchips, nanobots, or other tracking devices designed to monitor and control the population like some kind of medical dystopian nightmare.

The most popular version suggests Bill Gates, the World Health Organization, and various government agencies have inserted microscopic chips into vaccines to track people's movements, monitor their health data, or even control their thoughts and behavior. Nothing says "evil mastermind" like a guy who spent decades making computer software and now wants to prevent diseases.

Some believers extend this to include 5G cellular networks, claiming the microchips interact with 5G signals to enable remote mind control, population surveillance, or even targeted assassination through electromagnetic radiation. They point to the rollout of 5G networks during the pandemic as evidence of coordination between telecommunications companies and vaccine manufacturers. The timing of technological advancement during a global crisis is clearly suspicious and not just unfortunate coincidence.

The most extreme versions propose this is part of a global depopulation agenda, where the elite plan to kill or control most of humanity through this vaccine-chip-5G system. They cite patents filed by tech companies for various biometric technologies as "proof" such systems exist and are being implemented through vaccination programs, completely missing the distinction between filing a patent and secretly implanting mind control devices in your shoulder.

Why It's Asinine

Basic technology makes this impossible. Microchips small enough to fit through a vaccine needle would be smaller than a grain of rice. Current microchip technology at that size has extremely limited functionality: basic RFID chips can store a few bytes of information and require close-range readers to function. These chips enabling GPS tracking, mind control, or complex data transmission is pure science fiction.

If governments wanted to track people, they wouldn't need to secretly inject chips when everyone voluntarily carries smartphones with GPS, cameras, microphones, and internet connectivity. Your phone tracks your location, purchases, communications, and browsing habits with far greater precision than any theoretical microchip could achieve. Shadowy conspirators going through the enormous complexity of a global vaccination program when people literally post their locations on social media is laughably inefficient.

The 5G connection makes even less sense. 5G operates at specific frequencies having nothing to do with controlling microchips or human behavior. The electromagnetic radiation from 5G towers is non-ionizing and far too weak to cause biological effects at the distances involved. If 5G could control people's minds, wouldn't we have noticed obvious behavioral changes in areas with 5G coverage?

The sheer logistics of such a conspiracy would be impossible to maintain. You'd need every vaccine manufacturer, researcher, regulatory agency, healthcare worker, and government official worldwide to be in on it.

That's millions of people keeping the same secret across dozens of countries with vastly different political systems. Meanwhile, these same conspirators can't keep anything else secret.

My Commentary

The vaccine microchip conspiracy might be the perfect example of how ignorance breeds confidence. These people will confidently lecture you about nanotechnology and electromagnetic frequencies while clearly having no idea how either works. Imagine someone explaining how cars work by insisting they're powered by tiny hamsters running on wheels under the hood.

The selective skepticism is infuriating. These folks question every aspect of vaccine development but completely trust anonymous social media posts and YouTube videos made by people whose scientific credentials include "I did my own research." They demand peer-reviewed evidence for vaccine safety but accept blurry videos of keys supposedly sticking to arms as definitive proof of magnetic microchips.

The irony is delicious. People posting these theories on Facebook from their smartphones are worried about government tracking through vaccines. They're using devices tracking their every move while panicking about theoretical chips far less capable of surveillance than the computers they carry voluntarily in their pockets.

The real cost is concrete: this conspiracy has led people to refuse vaccines saving their lives or their children's lives. We're watching preventable diseases return because people are more afraid of imaginary microchips than actual viruses.

What They Believe

Homeopathy, developed by German physician Samuel Hahnemann in 1796, is based on two principles contradicting everything we know about chemistry, biology, and physics. The "law of similars" claims substances causing symptoms in healthy people can cure those same symptoms in sick people when properly diluted. The "law of infinitesimals" holds that the more you dilute a substance, the more potent it becomes medicinally.

Homeopathic remedies are created through "serial dilution" and "succussion" (vigorous shaking), like the world's most elaborate cocktail preparation resulting in a drink with no alcohol. A substance is diluted 1:10 or 1:100 repeatedly, with vigorous shaking between each dilution. Common dilutions like "30C" mean the original substance was diluted 1:100 thirty times, resulting in a final dilution of 1 part original substance to 10^{60} parts water. At this level, it's astronomically unlikely that even a single molecule of the original substance remains.

Homeopaths claim water retains a "memory" of substances it once contained, even after dilution removes all traces of the original material. They believe this water memory becomes stronger with each dilution and shaking, somehow imprinting the water with the "energetic signature" of the original substance. Water is clearly much smarter than we give it credit for.

Why It's Asinine

If water had memory as homeopaths claim, every glass of water would be a complex homeopathic remedy containing the memory of every substance it ever contacted: fish waste, industrial chemicals, dinosaur urine, and countless other materials cycled through the water system for billions of years. Homeopaths can't explain why water selectively remembers only the substances they want it to remember.

The dilutions used in homeopathy are so extreme they defy comprehension. A 30C dilution contains one part original substance in 10^{60} parts water. To put this in perspective, this is like dissolving one molecule in a sphere of water with a diameter larger than the distance from Earth to the Sun. Most homeopathic remedies contain literally nothing but water and sugar pills.

Extensive scientific testing has consistently shown homeopathic remedies perform no better than placebo in treating any condition. When studies are properly controlled for bias and random error, the apparent effects of homeopathy disappear faster than a magician's rabbit.

My Commentary

Homeopathy might be the most successful placebo industry in human history. It's brilliant in its simplicity: take water, remove everything having any possible effect, shake it up, and sell it as medicine. It's like starting a restaurant that serves empty plates and convincing customers they're just not sophisticated enough to taste the invisible food.

Homeopathy exploits people's legitimate concerns about modern medicine while offering literally nothing in return. People worry about side effects from real medicines, so they turn to treatments working by containing no medicine whatsoever. It's like being afraid of getting wet in the rain so you stand under a dry umbrella during a drought, except you're paying premium prices for the privilege.

The water memory claims are especially rich coming from people who often can't remember where they put their car keys five minutes ago. They're certain water can retain complex molecular memories of healing substances while simultaneously forgetting that the same water has been through countless animals, sewage systems, and industrial processes.

What They Believe

Crystal healing practitioners claim crystals and gemstones possess special energetic properties healing physical ailments, balancing emotional states, and enhancing spiritual well-being, basically turning your local rock shop into a supernatural pharmacy. They believe different crystals vibrate at specific frequencies interacting with the human body's supposed energy fields or "chakras" to restore health and harmony.

Practitioners assign specific healing properties to different stones with the confidence of someone reading from a cosmic menu: amethyst for anxiety and addiction, rose quartz for emotional healing and love, clear quartz as a general amplifier, black tourmaline for protection from negative energy, and citrine for prosperity and confidence. They use crystals by placing them on or around the body, wearing them as jewelry, carrying them in pockets, creating crystal grids, or infusing water with crystal energy for drinking. Water can be improved by proximity to pretty rocks.

Energy medicine extends beyond crystals to include practices like Reiki, therapeutic touch, and chakra balancing. Practitioners claim they can manipulate invisible energy fields around the human body to promote healing, which would be impressive if these energy fields existed in the first place.

Why It's Asinine

Crystals have no special properties beyond their physical and chemical characteristics. They're collections of atoms arranged in specific geometric patterns, nothing more. They emit healing energy, vibrate at therapeutic frequencies, or interact with human energy fields has no basis in physics, chemistry, or biology.

If crystals could heal through energy or vibrations, we'd be able to detect and measure these effects using scientific instruments. We have incredibly sensitive devices detecting electromagnetic radiation, magnetic fields, and other forms of energy at levels far below what would be needed for therapeutic effects. Yet no one has ever detected any unusual energy emissions from healing crystals differing from ordinary rocks.

The supposed chakra system crystal healing relies upon has no anatomical basis. There are no energy centers in the human body corresponding to chakra locations, no energy pathways matching meridian maps, and no scientific evidence for human auras or energy fields.

Scientific testing of crystal healing consistently shows it performs no better than placebo. When people can't tell whether they're holding real crystals or fake ones, the supposed healing effects disappear faster than free food at a college event.

My Commentary

Crystal healing might be the most beautifully absurd medical belief system ever devised. It combines the allure of pretty rocks with the promise of magical healing, creating a perfect storm of wishful thinking and geological ignorance. Imagine believing that collecting fancy pebbles makes you a doctor, except with more expensive pebbles and fancier terminology.

Crystal healers can look at a chunk of quartz (literally one of the most common minerals on Earth) and convince themselves it's a sophisticated medical device. Quartz makes up a significant percentage of ordinary sand and gravel, yet somehow becomes a miracle cure when polished and sold in a wellness shop with mystical lighting. If crystals really had healing properties, every beach would be a hospital and every gravel driveway would be a medical center.

The energy field claims are especially hilarious when you consider these same people use smartphones, Wi-Fi, and other electronic devices emitting measurable electromagnetic radiation. They're surrounded by real energy fields every day but somehow can't detect them, yet they're certain they can feel the "vibrations" from a polished rock sitting on their nightstand.

What They Believe

Miracle Mineral Solution (MMS) and chlorine dioxide protocol (CDS) advocates claim drinking diluted bleach solutions can cure virtually any disease, from autism and cancer to HIV and COVID-19, basically turning household cleaning products into the world's most dangerous pharmacy. The primary promoter, Jim Humble, claimed he discovered MMS while gold prospecting in South America, where he allegedly used water purification drops to cure malaria in his team. Nothing says "medical breakthrough" like a prospector inventing medicine while looking for shiny rocks.

MMS consists of sodium chlorite mixed with an acid activator (usually citric acid), creating chlorine dioxide, a powerful industrial bleaching agent and disinfectant normally used to clean swimming pools and treat sewage. Advocates claim this solution works by "oxidizing" pathogens in the body, killing viruses, bacteria, fungi, and parasites while somehow leaving healthy cells unharmed.

Believers follow detailed protocols involving increasingly concentrated doses of MMS taken multiple times per day, often accompanied by enemas and topical applications. Some extend the treatment to children and pets, claiming it can cure autism by "detoxifying" heavy metals and pathogens from the body. They interpret severe side effects like nausea, vomiting, and diarrhea as "detox reactions" or "pathogen die-off" instead of signs of chemical poisoning.

Why It's Asinine

Chlorine dioxide is an industrial disinfectant — the same chemical used to clean swimming pools and treat sewage — which should be your first clue it's not intended for human consumption. That a substance powerful enough to kill bacteria and viruses in industrial settings would somehow differentiate between "good" and "bad" cells in the human body defies basic chemistry and biology.

The human body maintains delicate chemical balances disrupted by consuming oxidizing agents. Chlorine dioxide causes chemical burns to mucous membranes, damages red blood cells, and can lead to severe dehydration, electrolyte imbalances, and organ failure. The symptoms MMS advocates dismiss as "detox reactions" are signs of chemical poisoning.

There is no scientific evidence MMS can treat any medical condition. No peer-reviewed research supports any therapeutic use of MMS in humans, while numerous case reports document serious injuries and deaths from consumption.

The FDA has issued multiple warnings about MMS, documented numerous hospitalizations, and prosecuted distributors for selling unapproved drugs. Poison control centers regularly receive calls about MMS poisoning, especially involving children whose parents gave them bleach thinking it was medicine.

My Commentary

The MMS movement represents perhaps the most dangerous intersection of medical ignorance and parental desperation in this entire book, and it makes me genuinely angry. These people are literally giving bleach to their children while convincing themselves they're providing healing instead of poisoning.

The mental gymnastics required to interpret chemical burns as healing is mind-boggling. When your child develops severe diarrhea, vomiting, and dehydration after drinking bleach, and you convince yourself these are "detox symptoms," you've entered a level of denial making professional magicians jealous.

This movement targets vulnerable populations, especially parents of autistic children. These families are often dealing with significant stress and limited resources, and along comes someone selling them false hope in a bottle of industrial disinfectant. Picture running a con game in a pediatric oncology ward, except somehow even more morally bankrupt.

Children have died because their parents chose bleach instead of medical treatment. When someone's child has a serious illness and they waste precious time giving them pool chemicals instead of seeking real medical care, the consequences can be irreversible.

What They Believe

Urine therapy practitioners believe drinking your own urine or applying it topically can cure diseases, boost immunity, and promote overall health and longevity, basically turning your bathroom into a health spa and your bladder into a medicine cabinet. They claim urine contains valuable nutrients, hormones, enzymes, and antibodies wasted when eliminated from the body.

Believers practice various forms: drinking fresh morning urine (considered most potent), consuming aged or fermented urine for enhanced effects, using urine enemas or douches, applying urine to skin conditions, or even injecting urine subcutaneously. Some practitioners follow elaborate protocols involving fasting, specific timing, and gradual dose increases to maximize supposed benefits.

Advanced practitioners claim different urine streams have different properties: first morning urine for detoxification, midstream for general health. They believe urine from healthy people can treat illness in others, leading to urine sharing networks and even urine banking for future medical use.

Why It's Asinine

Urine is waste. That's literally its entire biological purpose: to remove toxins, excess water, and metabolic byproducts the body needs to eliminate. The kidneys filter blood to extract these unwanted substances and expel them from the body. Drinking urine forces the kidneys to process the same waste products repeatedly, creating unnecessary stress on these vital organs.

The composition of urine varies dramatically based on hydration, diet, medications, and health status, making any supposed therapeutic effects completely unpredictable. When someone is sick, their urine often contains higher concentrations of toxins and waste products their body is trying to eliminate. Consuming this concentrated waste is like eating garbage because you're hungry, except garbage might be more nutritious.

While urine is sterile when produced by healthy kidneys, it quickly becomes contaminated with bacteria once it leaves the body. Drinking aged or fermented urine exposes people to potentially dangerous bacterial infections.

There is no credible scientific evidence supporting any health benefits from urine consumption. Studies examining urine composition focus on diagnostic applications, not therapeutic uses. The medical literature contains only case reports of urine therapy causing harm.

My Commentary

Urine therapy might represent the ultimate triumph of wishful thinking against basic common sense. These people have convinced themselves their bodily waste is a health elixir, turning the bathroom into a pharmacy and making every trip to the toilet a potential health opportunity. It's like believing garbage trucks are food delivery services operating in reverse.

The rationalization required to believe kidneys (organs designed to remove unwanted substances from the body) are concentrating medicine for consumption is breathtaking. Imagine believing sewage treatment plants are gourmet food processing facilities and we've been wasting perfectly good cuisine by flushing it away.

The claims about ancient wisdom are especially amusing given that people throughout history tried all sorts of desperate measures when facing illness or death. Just because someone 2,000 years ago tried drinking urine doesn't mean it was effective, it means they were desperate and didn't have access to medicine.

When your health strategy involves drinking the stuff your body tried to get rid of, you might want to reconsider your approach to wellness.

Chapter 3: Celebrity Immortality Club

Chapter Introduction

Welcome to the world of people who can't accept that famous people die like everyone else, so they've convinced themselves that death is just a really elaborate career move. This chapter explores humans who believe celebrities fake their own deaths and then spend decades living secret lives, presumably because nothing says "retirement planning" like convincing the entire world you're dead while secretly buying groceries in disguise.

We're covering four entries, and they escalate. The Elvis theory is at least emotionally coherent — the man was beloved, his death was sudden, and grief does strange things to people. Tupac's version requires a little more gymnastics. Paul McCartney's is so logically broken it accidentally proves the opposite of what believers intend. And Michael Jackson's is the one that stops being funny when you think about his kids.

The common thread is what these theories do to the people they're supposedly honoring. Every single one transforms its subject from a flawed human being into a coward who chose to abandon everyone who loved them rather than face their problems. That's not fan devotion. That's something darker dressed up as devotion.

What They Believe

Elvis believers claim the King of Rock and Roll didn't die on August 16, 1977, but instead faked his death to escape fame pressures, financial troubles, or organized crime threats. According to this theory, Elvis staged his death with FBI help (federal agents moonlight as celebrity death consultants) and has been living in hiding ever since, presumably perfecting his peanut butter and banana sandwich recipes in rural obscurity.

Believers point to supposed "evidence": Elvis sightings everywhere from Burger King restaurants to remote islands, photographs of men who vaguely resemble Elvis if you squint really hard, and supposed inconsistencies in his death certificate and autopsy reports. They claim "Elvis" on the death certificate is misspelled as "Aaron" instead of "Aron" (his middle name), proving the whole death was faked instead of demonstrating that even death certificates can have typos.

Some versions suggest Elvis became a DEA agent and faked his death to go undercover. Nothing says "deep cover operation" like being the most recognizable face in America. Others believe he's living on a secret island, in witness protection, or quietly enjoying retirement in a small town where nobody recognizes him, despite Elvis impersonators existing because his look is so recognizable.

Why It's Asinine

Here's the problem nobody in the Elvis-is-alive community wants to address: he was visibly dying for years before 1977. This wasn't a man in his prime who vanished at the peak of his powers. Elvis's final concert performances are on YouTube. Go watch them. He was bloated, slurring lyrics, barely able to move, propped up by prescription drugs that were destroying him in real time. His doctor was prescribing him so many controlled substances that the sheer volume later became a legal scandal.

So the theory asks us to believe that all of this — the weight gain, the pill dependency, the deteriorating performances — was an elaborate setup for faking his death. Elvis spent years poisoning himself and humiliating himself on stage as the opening act to his own disappearing act. That's the plan? Most people planning to fake their death don't spend the preceding years making themselves look as bad as possible in front of thousands of witnesses.

The "evidence" is what you'd expect: a typo on a death certificate, blurry photos of elderly men, and sightings at Burger Kings across the American South. The typo — "Aaron" instead of "Aron" — proves that even death certificates have clerical errors, which is not a conspiracy and is also not interesting. The Burger King sightings prove that some older heavyset men with sideburns exist, which is also not a conspiracy and is also not interesting.

Every doctor, nurse, family member, and funeral professional who was present would need to have maintained perfect silence for nearly fifty years. These are the same people who couldn't keep his prescription drug problem secret when he was alive.

My Commentary

Of all the beliefs in this chapter, Elvis is the one I can't fully mock. The man died at 42 from the consequences of addiction and the pressures of a fame he'd had since he was a teenager. His death was preventable. The people around him failed him. And when it happened, millions of people who had loved his music since childhood found themselves unable to process it.

I understand why "he got away" is more bearable than "the system chewed him up and spat him out." One is a story with a survivor. The other is just a tragedy.

But the believers are doing something strange with their love. The alive-Elvis theory requires him to have spent nearly fifty years as a nobody, cut off from music, performing, family, everything that defined him — while the people who loved him grieved publicly. That's not an escape. That's a different kind of death. And it turns the King of Rock and Roll into someone who thought his own comfort was worth more than his daughter's father.

Tupac's Secret Life

What They Believe

Tupac believers claim the rapper didn't die from gunshot wounds on September 13, 1996, but instead faked his death to escape the dangerous East Coast-West Coast hip-hop rivalry, legal troubles, or death threats from enemies. According to this theory, Tupac staged his shooting in Las Vegas with the help of associates and has been living in hiding ever since, presumably working on the world's longest album delay while perfecting his disguise techniques.

Believers point to supposed "evidence": the symbolism in Tupac's final album title "The Don Killuminati: The 7 Day Theory" (released under the alias Makaveli), his interest in political philosopher Niccolò Machiavelli who wrote about faking one's death, and his quick cremation after death, destroying evidence of the hoax. They interpret song lyrics as coded messages about his planned disappearance and claim various music videos contain hidden clues about his survival.

Some versions suggest Tupac fled to Cuba, where he's living under political protection, or that he's hiding in other countries where he can't be extradited. Others believe he's living secretly in the United States, occasionally releasing new music through intermediaries or making coded appearances in other artists' work. The most elaborate theories incorporate supposed sightings of Tupac in various locations, often involving blurry photographs or security camera footage of men who might look like an older Tupac if you really want them to.

Why It's Asinine

Forget the medical records for a moment. Forget the hospital staff, the autopsy, the police reports, all of it. Just think about who Tupac Shakur actually was.

This was a man who got shot in a New York recording studio lobby in 1994, was hit five times, and gave a press conference from his hospital bed the next day wearing a do-rag and a hospital gown, refusing to let anyone see him as a victim. He spent his entire public life refusing to back down from anything. He made records about police brutality while under federal surveillance. He was awaiting a sexual assault verdict when he recorded some of his most politically charged music. Running away from danger was not in his character at any observable point in his life.

So the theory asks us to believe that this same man — shot multiple times in Las Vegas, which was genuinely dangerous and genuinely connected to real people who genuinely wanted him dead — decided his response would be to fake his death, flee to Cuba, and spend the rest of his life in silence. Not fight back. Not make more music. Not continue the social justice work he talked about constantly. Just disappear quietly and let everyone think he was gone. The most outspoken artist of his generation supposedly chose silence. Forever. Because that tracks.

The Machiavelli angle is a particular favorite of believers and a good example of how pattern recognition misfires. Tupac read Machiavelli in prison and used Makaveli as an alias. Machiavelli wrote about strategic deception. Therefore Tupac faked his death. By this logic, anyone who has read The Count of Monte Cristo is planning a prison escape, and anyone who has seen The Prestige is currently sawing themselves in half.

My Commentary

Tupac would now be in his mid-fifties. Believers are arguing he's spent more years in hiding than he spent alive. They're claiming that one of the most outspoken men in American music — someone who genuinely risked his life to say things that needed saying — made a calculated decision to go permanently silent at 25 and just stayed silent. For three decades. While the violence and injustice he rapped about continued without him.

There's something almost insulting about that story. It takes everything Tupac stood for and replaces it with cowardice dressed up as cleverness. The real ending — a 25-year-old killed by the exact kind of senseless street violence he'd been documenting his entire career — is tragic precisely because it meant something. The fake-death version means nothing. He just left.

His death should have been a reckoning. In some circles it was. But the conspiracy theory turned it into a puzzle box, and people have been staring at the box for thirty years instead of dealing with what's inside it.

What They Believe

Paul is Dead theorists claim Paul McCartney died in a car crash in November 1966 and was secretly replaced by a lookalike named William "Billy" Campbell (or various other names depending on which version you follow). According to this conspiracy, The Beatles, their management, and record label decided to cover up Paul's death to prevent mass hysteria among fans and protect their commercial interests. Nothing says "business as usual" like replacing your bassist with a random guy and hoping nobody notices.

Believers claim The Beatles left coded clues about Paul's death throughout their later albums: supposed backward messages when songs are played in reverse, symbolic imagery in album artwork, and lyrical references to death and replacement. They point to the Abbey Road album cover, where Paul appears barefoot and out of step with the other Beatles, as representing a funeral procession with Paul as the corpse.

The theory incorporates supposed physical differences between the "real" Paul and his replacement: changes in height, facial features, and left-handedness becoming right-handedness (ignoring that Paul remained left-handed throughout his career). Believers analyze photographs with the intensity of forensic investigators, claiming to find evidence of plastic surgery, different ear shapes, and height discrepancies somehow escaping the notice of everyone who knew Paul personally.

Why It's Asinine

Let's grant the theory everything it wants. Paul McCartney died in November 1966. The Beatles secretly replaced him with a man named Billy Campbell, who had somehow mastered Paul's voice, his left-handed bass playing, his melodic instincts, and his ability to fool everyone who had known Paul since childhood — including Paul's family, his girlfriends, and three men who had been his closest friends since their teenage years in Liverpool. Fine. Now look at what Billy Campbell proceeded to do.

"Hello Goodbye." "Penny Lane." "Eleanor Rigby" backing vocals. The entire Let It Be album. "Hey Jude," which remains one of the best-selling singles in recorded history. "The Long and Winding Road." Wings. "Band on the Run." "Maybe I'm Amazed." A solo career spanning six decades that includes some of the most recognized songs ever written, performed live into his eighties with the same voice and the same left-handed Höfner bass.

The Paul is Dead theory has accidentally constructed an argument that Paul McCartney's replacement was a superior musician to Paul McCartney. Billy Campbell, a random man who apparently materialized in 1966 with no prior public existence, turned out to be one of the most talented composers of the 20th century. The Beatles didn't lose anything when Paul died. They upgraded.

This is where the theory collapses under its own weight. Believers spend so much energy on the backward audio and the barefoot Abbey Road walk that they never stop to address the central absurdity: the theory requires Paul's replacement to have been brilliant enough to fool the world for sixty years while producing some of the greatest pop music ever made. At some point you have to ask whether you're mourning the original Paul or quietly rooting for Billy.

My Commentary

Paul McCartney is currently 82 years old, still touring, still performing three-hour shows, still writing songs, still legally winning copyright disputes over music he co-wrote in the 1960s from memory. He has recalled specific anecdotes from his childhood in Liverpool, his early friendship with John Lennon, and sessions at Abbey Road with a level of detail that forensic analysts would be hard pressed to fake.

Either Billy Campbell is the greatest long-term impersonation in human history — a method acting performance that has now lasted longer than most human lifespans — or Paul McCartney did not die in a car crash in 1966. I'm going to go ahead and say it's the second one.

The backward audio "evidence" is my personal favorite part of this mythology. Play "Revolution 9" in reverse and you can hear "Turn me on, dead man." You can also hear, depending on your commitment level, "we all live in a yellow submarine," "my sweet Lord," or whatever else your brain has decided it wants to find in twenty seconds of reversed tape hiss. This is not music analysis. This is audio Rorschach for people who need John Lennon to have been secretly signaling them from a 1968 recording studio.

What They Believe

Michael Jackson death hoax believers claim the King of Pop didn't die on June 25, 2009, but instead faked his death to escape financial troubles, legal problems, or the intense media scrutiny plaguing him for decades. According to this theory, Michael staged his death with help from his doctor, family members, or other associates and has been living in secret ever since, presumably practicing his moonwalk in private while the world mourns his loss.

Believers point to supposed "evidence": inconsistencies in the emergency call timeline, questions about his autopsy and death certificate, and alleged sightings of Michael at various locations around the world. They claim the ambulance photo showing a figure on a stretcher doesn't look like Michael, that his funeral was closed-casket to hide that the body wasn't really him, and that various family members and associates have made statements interpreted as coded admissions that Michael is still alive.

Some versions suggest Michael is living in Bahrain, where he had previously taken refuge, or that he's hiding on a private island owned by wealthy supporters. Others believe he's undergone plastic surgery to change his appearance (ignoring that he'd had extensive plastic surgery before his death) and is living anonymously in various countries. The most elaborate theories incorporate supposed sightings of Michael in disguise, often involving grainy surveillance footage or photographs of men who might look like Michael if you really want them to.

Why It's Asinine

Conrad Murray is in this. That's where the theory ends for me.

Michael's personal physician was convicted of involuntary manslaughter in 2011 for his role in Michael's death. He lost his medical license. He served two years in jail. If Michael Jackson faked his death, then Murray sat through an entire criminal trial — his own criminal trial, for a crime that destroyed his career and his freedom — without saying a word. He went to prison rather than explain that nobody actually died. That's not a cover-up. That's a man being convicted of killing someone who is dead.

The rest of the "evidence" is the standard package: grainy surveillance footage, closed casket, timeline inconsistencies, family members saying things that sound cryptic if you remove the surrounding context. None of it is evidence of anything except that people under extreme stress behave strangely, closed caskets happen, and surveillance cameras produce bad footage.

But here's the part that should stop the theory cold. Michael had three young children when he died — Prince was 12, Paris was 11, Blanket was 7. By all accounts, and by the testimony of people who knew him well, being their father was the most important thing in his life. He spent years in legal battles to maintain custody and protect them from media exposure. He shielded their faces in public. He restructured his entire life around them. The theory asks us to believe he looked at those three kids and chose to let them grow up thinking their father was dead. That's not a theory about a man escaping his problems. That's a theory about a man who didn't love his children.

My Commentary

The Michael Jackson death hoax community has been active for fifteen years now, and the longer it runs, the more clearly you can see what it actually is: people processing shock by converting grief into detective work. His death was genuinely unexpected. He'd just announced a comeback tour. He was 50. Nobody saw it coming. I'm not unsympathetic to that disorientation. But fifteen years is long enough.

Michael Jackson died from acute propofol intoxication administered by a doctor who was more interested in keeping a paying client happy than in keeping him alive. That's a story about the toxicity of extreme celebrity, about the people who surround the very famous and enable their worst impulses while calling it care. It's a story that matters and that keeps repeating itself — Elvis, Heath Ledger, Prince, Michael — and we never seem to learn anything from it because we're too busy deciding whether the guy in the blurry airport footage has the right jawline.

Meanwhile, his three children grew up without their father. Paris Jackson has spoken publicly about her grief and her mental health struggles. That's what's real. That's what the death hoax community is looking away from when it zooms in on ambulance photos and parses interview transcripts for coded admissions.

He's gone. The people who loved him are still here. Pay attention to them.

Chapter 4: Secret Societies and Shadow Governments

Chapter Introduction

Somewhere between a broken world and human psychology's desperate need for it to make sense sits the conspiracy theory. This chapter is about people who can't accept that incompetence explains most of history, so they've decided that secret organizations explain it instead.

We're diving into six spectacular examples of people who mistake correlation for causation and assume malice where incompetence would suffice: Illuminati believers (everything bad is planned by a secret society founded in 1776), Bilderberg Group paranoia (rich people meeting annually to discuss world domination instead of just networking), New World Order fantasies (one world government is coming to take your guns and freedom), Reptilian overlords (shape-shifting lizard aliens secretly rule humanity), Royal Family lizard theories (the British monarchy are literally cold-blooded), and celebrity lizard spotting (Hollywood is full of badly disguised reptiles).

These beliefs aren't just detached from how power works in the modern world. They require believing that incompetent governments who can't fix potholes or deliver mail on time are somehow capable of maintaining perfect secrecy across centuries while orchestrating elaborate global conspiracies. These folks have convinced themselves that everything from natural disasters to their morning coffee being cold is part of a master plan instead of accepting that the world is mostly random chaos punctuated by human stupidity.

The psychology involves pattern-seeking, the need for control, and the comforting delusion that someone somewhere knows what they're doing. Pull up a chair. The lizard people are waiting.

What They Believe

Modern Illuminati conspiracy theorists claim a secret society founded in Bavaria in 1776 has survived for nearly 250 years and now controls world governments, financial systems, entertainment industries, and basically everything happening on Earth. According to believers, this shadowy organization orchestrates wars, economic crashes, political elections, natural disasters, and even pop culture trends as part of their master plan to establish a New World Order and enslave humanity under one global government.

Believers see Illuminati symbols everywhere: the all-seeing eye on the dollar bill, triangles in corporate logos, hand gestures by celebrities, and numerical patterns in dates of major events. They claim the Illuminati communicates through hidden messages in movies, music videos, and television shows, because apparently the best way to maintain a secret conspiracy is to constantly advertise your existence through popular media.

The supposed membership list includes every wealthy person, politician, celebrity, and business leader who has ever achieved success, because obviously talent, hard work, and luck have nothing to do with accomplishment. Instead, anyone who becomes famous or powerful must have sold their soul to the Illuminati in exchange for success, wealth, and the secret knowledge of how to make really good guacamole.

Modern versions incorporate ancient aliens, satanic rituals, blood sacrifices, mind control technology, and interdimensional beings, because a simple secret society wasn't exciting enough. Some believers claim the

Illuminati harvests adrenochrome from children, controls the weather, and stages mass shootings to promote gun control, turning every tragedy into evidence of the conspiracy.

Why It's Asinine

The historical Illuminati was a real organization founded by Adam Weishaupt in 1776 in Bavaria. It was a small Enlightenment-era society promoting reason, secular values, and opposition to religious influence in government. It had maybe 2,000 members at its peak, operated openly for about a decade, and was suppressed by the Bavarian government in 1785. That's it. No world domination, no centuries-spanning conspiracy, just a short-lived intellectual society shut down by local authorities.

This small, defunct organization somehow survived, grew into a global shadow government, and maintained perfect secrecy for 250 years while leaving obvious clues everywhere is logistically impossible. Real conspiracies involving more than a handful of people fall apart within months or years. The Manhattan Project, involving 130,000 people working on the atomic bomb during World War II, stayed secret for maybe three years before information started leaking.

The supposed "evidence" for Illuminati control consists entirely of coincidences, misinterpreted symbols, and connecting dots that don't connect. The all-seeing eye on the dollar bill? It's a Masonic symbol predating any Illuminati conspiracy theories. Triangles in corporate logos? Triangles are basic geometric shapes appearing in design because they're visually appealing and structurally stable, not because logo designers are secret society members.

If the Illuminati really controlled everything, they're doing a terrible job. Wars, economic crashes, pandemics, climate change, and countless other global problems suggest that either nobody's in charge or whoever is in charge is spectacularly incompetent. A secret organization orchestrating these disasters as part of their master plan makes them seem less like evil geniuses and more like cosmic sadists with really poor management skills.

My Commentary

The Illuminati conspiracy might be the most narcissistic delusion in human history, because it requires believing you're smart enough to detect a secret conspiracy fooling everyone else for centuries. These people think they've uncovered the truth about world events by watching YouTube videos and noticing that some logos contain triangles, which makes them feel like intellectual heroes fighting against the forces of evil with nothing but internet research and righteous indignation.

Believers claim to oppose a secret society seeking world domination while simultaneously promoting an ideology that divides the world into good guys (conspiracy believers) and bad guys (everyone else) — which is exactly the kind of us-versus-them thinking actual authoritarian movements run on. They're creating their own conspiracy to fight an imaginary one.

The pattern recognition here is so aggressive it borders on parody. These folks see Illuminati symbols in everything from pizza logos to stop signs, because apparently the secret rulers of the world are really bad at keeping secrets and constantly feel compelled to announce their presence through corporate branding. Think of a secret society so obsessed with marketing that they can't resist putting their logo on Taco Bell cups.

The opportunity cost is enormous. This conspiracy thinking prevents people from addressing real problems with real solutions. Instead of working on issues like corruption, inequality, or climate change, believers spend their time fighting an imaginary enemy while real problems get worse. It's like tilting at windmills, except Don Quixote had better pattern recognition skills.

What They Believe

Bilderberg Group conspiracy theorists claim this annual private conference of political leaders, business executives, and academics is a secret world government meeting where attendees decide global policy, plan economic crashes, choose world leaders, and coordinate international events. According to believers, the roughly 130 people who attend this three-day conference each year secretly control world affairs and use the meeting to coordinate their master plan for global domination.

Believers see the Bilderberg Group as proof of the New World Order conspiracy, claiming attendees make binding decisions about wars, elections, economic policies, and social changes then implemented worldwide. They point to the private nature of the meetings, the high-profile attendees, and the lack of official transcripts as evidence that world leaders are plotting against their own citizens instead of just networking and discussing global issues.

The conspiracy extends to claims that Bilderberg attendees choose presidents, prime ministers, and other world leaders in advance, making democratic elections meaningless theater designed to maintain the illusion of choice. Some versions suggest the group coordinates false flag operations, stages terrorist attacks, and manipulates financial markets to increase their power and wealth.

More extreme believers incorporate the Bilderberg Group into larger conspiracy theories involving the Illuminati, reptilian shapeshifters, and satanic rituals, because apparently rich people meeting annually to discuss global issues wasn't sinister enough without adding interdimensional lizard worship.

Why It's Asinine

The Bilderberg Group is not a secret organization plotting world domination. It's a private conference started in 1954 to encourage dialogue between Europe and North America during the Cold War. The meetings bring together politicians, business leaders, and academics to discuss global issues like economic policy, international relations, and technological development. Think of it as an exclusive networking event with really expensive catering and security.

The meetings are private to encourage open discussion, not to plot global conspiracies. Attendees don't make binding decisions or vote on world policy because they have no authority to do so. They're people representing different countries, political parties, and competing business interests. They could agree on a master plan for anything more complex than what to serve for lunch is laughably naive about how international relations work.

The supposed "evidence" for Bilderberg conspiracy theories consists mainly of the fact that powerful people meet privately and sometimes similar policies emerge in different countries afterward. This isn't evidence of conspiracy, it's evidence that people facing similar problems often reach similar solutions, especially when they've discussed those problems with experts and peers.

If the Bilderberg Group really controlled world events, they're spectacularly bad at it. The world is full of conflicts, economic instability, political disagreements, and competing national interests suggesting nobody's in charge of anything. Brexit happened despite most Bilderberg attendees opposing it. Trump won the US presidency despite not being the establishment choice.

Global cooperation on climate change has been painfully slow despite it being a regular Bilderberg topic.

My Commentary

The Bilderberg conspiracy perfectly illustrates how people mistake networking for mind control and assume malice where mundane explanation would suffice. These believers think that when powerful people meet to discuss global issues, they must be plotting something sinister, because clearly the only reason politicians and business leaders would talk to each other is to coordinate evil schemes instead of just doing their jobs.

The paranoia here requires believing that people who can't agree on basic policy within their own countries somehow coordinate perfectly across national boundaries to implement a global agenda. Have these conspiracy theorists ever tried to organize a dinner party with more than six people? Getting that many world leaders to agree on where to go for lunch would be an achievement, let alone coordinating a secret global government.

These people want more transparency and democratic accountability in global decision-making, which are reasonable goals. But instead of working through political processes, they've convinced themselves that everything is controlled by a secret cabal meeting in fancy hotels. That's like demanding open government by declaring city council meetings satanic rituals.

There's a basic logic problem here. These conspiracy theorists think the Bilderberg Group is so powerful it controls world events but so incompetent it can't keep its annual meeting secret despite having unlimited resources and global influence. Every year, the location, attendee list, and general topics are publicly announced, making it the least secret secret meeting in history.

What They Believe

New World Order conspiracy theorists claim a shadowy global elite is working to establish a single world government abolishing national sovereignty, eliminating individual freedoms, and enslaving humanity under totalitarian rule. According to believers, this conspiracy involves international organizations, multinational corporations, secret societies, and wealthy families coordinating across centuries to gradually erode national independence and personal liberty until they can impose their vision of global tyranny.

Believers point to international cooperation, trade agreements, global institutions, and diplomatic efforts as evidence of the conspiracy instead of normal responses to global challenges. They see the United Nations, European Union, World Economic Forum, and other international organizations as stepping stones toward world government instead of forums for addressing shared problems like climate change, economic instability, and international conflicts.

The supposed timeline varies wildly depending on which version you believe, with some claiming the New World Order will be implemented within years while others suggest it's a centuries-long gradual process. The methods allegedly include economic manipulation, manufactured crises, population control, mind control technology, and staged disasters designed to make people willingly surrender their freedoms in exchange for security and stability.

More elaborate versions incorporate religious prophecy, claiming the New World Order fulfills biblical predictions about the end times, the Antichrist, and the mark of the beast. Some believers think the conspiracy involves alien intervention, interdimensional beings, or time travelers working to reshape human civilization according to their mysterious agenda.

Why It's Asinine

The practical problems with establishing a world government are so enormous they make the logistics of organizing a family reunion look simple by comparison. Countries can barely cooperate on basic issues like trade agreements or environmental protection, let alone surrender their sovereignty to a global authority. Brexit happened because people couldn't tolerate being part of a voluntary economic union with their neighbors, but somehow a secret cabal is going to convince everyone to accept world government?

International organizations like the UN are notoriously ineffective precisely because they lack real authority over member nations. Countries routinely ignore UN resolutions, violate international law, and prioritize national interests over global cooperation. These same organizations are secretly powerful enough to impose world government contradicts everything we observe about how international relations work.

The supposed "evidence" for New World Order conspiracy theories consists mainly of normal international cooperation being reinterpreted as sinister plotting. Climate change agreements become population control schemes. Trade deals become sovereignty surrenders. Diplomatic negotiations become conspiracy meetings. It's like watching someone interpret a neighborhood watch meeting as evidence of a communist takeover.

If there really were a coordinated effort to establish world government, it would require unprecedented cooperation between groups that hate each other, perfect secrecy across thousands of people and organizations, and flawless execution of incredibly complex long-term plans. Meanwhile, these same conspirators can't coordinate basic responses to global crises or prevent information leaks from much simpler operations.

My Commentary

The New World Order conspiracy might be the most politically convenient delusion ever invented, because it allows people to blame all their problems on a shadowy enemy while avoiding the hard work of engaging with real political processes. Don't like globalization? Blame the New World Order. Worried about economic inequality? Secret global elite. Frustrated with complex international problems? Obviously it's all planned by evil conspirators.

This conspiracy thinking prevents people from understanding how power works in the modern world. Real influence comes from money, lobbying, campaign contributions, and political connections operating through transparent (if flawed) democratic processes. The wealthy and powerful don't need secret conspiracies to advance their interests when they can do it openly through perfectly legal means.

They claim to oppose tyranny while promoting an ideology that divides the world into good guys (patriots who see the truth) and bad guys (everyone who disagrees with them). That's not opposition to authoritarianism. That's the opening paragraph of authoritarianism. Arguing that democracy is fake and only you understand what's really happening is pretty much the foundation of every tyrannical movement in history.

Meanwhile, this conspiracy prevents people from addressing real problems with real solutions. Instead of working to improve democratic institutions, reduce corruption, or increase transparency, believers spend their time fighting an imaginary enemy while issues get worse. It's like refusing medical treatment because you think doctors are part of a conspiracy to make you sick.

What They Believe

Reptilian conspiracy theorists, popularized by former BBC sports broadcaster David Icke, claim that shape-shifting reptilian aliens secretly control human civilization by disguising themselves as world leaders, celebrities, and other powerful figures. According to this theory, these interdimensional lizard beings have been manipulating human society for thousands of years, breeding with humans to create hybrid bloodlines and using advanced technology to maintain their disguises while feeding off human energy and negative emotions.

Believers claim they can identify reptilians by looking for "tells" in their human disguises: vertical pupil slits, unusual blinking patterns, cold skin temperature, inability to show genuine human emotions, and occasional "glitches" where their reptilian features briefly become visible. They analyze photographs and videos of politicians and celebrities with the intensity of forensic investigators, claiming to spot evidence of scales, forked tongues, or inhuman facial features.

The supposed reptilian bloodlines include most royal families, political dynasties, and wealthy elites, because apparently the best way to secretly control humanity is to put yourself in highly visible public positions where millions of people can scrutinize your every move. Some versions suggest these beings are from another planet, another dimension, or the hollow interior of Earth, because the specific origin story matters less than the basic premise that lizard people are running everything.

More elaborate theories incorporate ancient aliens, suggesting reptilians have been influencing human civilization since ancient times and are responsible for creating religions, governments, and social structures designed to keep humans docile and easily controlled. Some believers think reptilians harvest human emotions, especially fear and suffering, as a form of sustenance or energy source.

Why It's Asinine

The basic premise requires believing that advanced alien beings capable of interdimensional travel and perfect shape-shifting technology chose to use their incredible abilities to... govern human beings and deal with budget committees, voter complaints, and media scrutiny. If you had the power to traverse dimensions and change your appearance at will, would you really choose to spend your time in city council meetings arguing about parking meter rates?

The supposed "evidence" for reptilian features in photographs and videos is explained by camera artifacts, compression algorithms, lighting effects, and the simple fact that high-definition cameras can make anyone look slightly inhuman under the wrong conditions. Believers are analyzing digital noise and calling it proof of alien infiltration, like concluding that static on your TV proves ghosts are trying to communicate.

The logistics of maintaining perfect disguises across thousands of people for thousands of years while leaving enough "tells" for conspiracy theorists to detect makes no sense. Either these beings are incredibly advanced and their disguises would be perfect, or they're incompetent enough to be detected by people watching YouTube videos on their phones. You can't have both master race genetic manipulation and obvious reptilian slips visible to amateur video analysts.

If reptilians really controlled human civilization, they're doing a terrible job of it. Wars, climate change, economic instability, and countless other problems suggest that whoever's in charge either doesn't know what they're doing or has the worst management philosophy in galactic history. Advanced aliens spending thousands of years creating the current mess we call human civilization is arguably more insulting to the reptilians than to us.

My Commentary

The reptilian conspiracy might be the most beautifully absurd theory in this entire book, because it combines every paranoid fantasy into one spectacular package of cosmic nonsense. It's got aliens, shape-shifters, ancient conspiracies, government control, and dimensional travel all wrapped up in a theory somehow making less sense than any of its individual components. It's like someone threw every conspiracy theory into a blender and hit the "maximum crazy" setting.

The visual analysis these believers do is amazing in its creativity. They'll spend hours examining photographs for evidence of reptilian features, finding scales where there are shadows, serpent eyes where there are camera glints, and forked tongues where there are normal human speech patterns. It's like the world's most elaborate game of "spot the difference," except the differences exist only in their imagination.

The social implications are fascinating too, because this conspiracy allows believers to dehumanize political opponents by literally claiming they're not human. Don't like a politician? They're not just wrong, they're a different species. It's the ultimate ad hominem attack: your argument is invalid because you're secretly a lizard from another dimension.

The theory collapses on one question: if these beings can traverse dimensions and maintain disguises for millennia, why do they keep getting caught on phone cameras by teenagers in basements? The theory requires believing that beings advanced enough to travel between dimensions and maintain perfect disguises for millennia somehow can't figure out how to avoid being detected by people with basic video editing software and too much time on their hands. Either we're dealing with the most incompetent advanced alien species in the universe, or maybe, just maybe, politicians look weird in photos because they're awkward humans who spend too much time under artificial lighting.

What They Believe

Royal reptilian conspiracy theorists claim the British Royal Family are shape-shifting lizard beings who have maintained their bloodline for centuries because they're not human. According to believers, the Windsor family (and most other European royal houses) are part of the reptilian elite secretly controlling humanity, using their positions as constitutional monarchs to coordinate global policies while hiding their true alien nature behind centuries of royal protocol and media management.

Believers analyze royal photographs, public appearances, and official portraits for evidence of reptilian features, claiming to spot unusual eye movements, scales visible under makeup, and behavioral patterns suggesting non-human psychology. They point to the family's longevity, political influence, and wealth as evidence that they possess alien advantages instead of the benefits of hereditary privilege, excellent healthcare, and institutional power.

The conspiracy extends to claims that royal bloodlines are maintained through intermarriage to preserve reptilian genetics, explaining why European royalty historically married within a limited circle of families. Some versions suggest that Princess Diana discovered the royal family's reptilian nature and was murdered to prevent her from exposing the truth, turning a tragic car accident into evidence of alien cover-up.

More elaborate theories incorporate the Royal Family into larger reptilian control structures, claiming they coordinate with other reptilian bloodlines around the world to maintain global control through a network of monarchies, governments, and secret societies. Some believers think royal ceremonies, coronations, and state functions are reptilian rituals designed to maintain their power and feed off human energy.

Why It's Asinine

The British Royal Family is one of the most photographed, scrutinized, and documented families in human history. Every public appearance is recorded by dozens of cameras, analyzed by media outlets, and watched by millions of people worldwide. If they were shape-shifting reptilians occasionally slipping back into lizard form, someone would have captured definitive evidence by now instead of grainy photos interpreted as anything.

The supposed "evidence" for royal reptilian features consists entirely of photographic artifacts, unusual expressions, and the simple fact that formal royal portraits often make people look stiff and unnatural because that's literally the point of formal royal portraiture. The Royal Family looks weird in official photos because they're posing according to centuries-old traditions designed to project dignity and authority, not because they're secretly lizards.

Royal intermarriage was about political alliances, territorial claims, and preventing civil wars over succession. European royalty married within limited circles because there were limited circles of people with appropriate social status and political value, not because they were trying to preserve alien genetics.

If the Royal Family were really reptilian overlords secretly controlling global affairs, they're remarkably bad at it given that the British Empire collapsed, the monarchy has minimal political power, and the current generation spends most of their time cutting ribbons at hospital openings and dealing with tabloid scandals about their personal lives.

My Commentary

The royal reptilian conspiracy might be the most culturally specific delusion in this book, because it requires a fundamental misunderstanding of how constitutional monarchy works in the modern world. These believers think the Royal Family secretly controls global affairs when their political power is roughly equivalent to that of a ceremonial mascot with excellent healthcare benefits and really expensive hats.

The visual analysis here is creative, because believers are arguing that centuries of formal royal portraiture, designed to make people look imposing and otherworldly, is evidence that these people are literally otherworldly. It's like concluding that opera singers are aliens because they sound inhuman when they're performing, while ignoring that sounding inhuman is the entire point of opera.

The Diana conspiracy angle is especially tragic, because it takes a genuinely heartbreaking accident and turns it into evidence of alien cover-up instead of acknowledging the simple reality that paparazzi harassment, dangerous driving, and mechanical failure can have fatal consequences. It's grief and conspiracy thinking combining to create a narrative somehow more comforting than accepting that sometimes terrible things just happen.

What's actually funny is that this conspiracy flatters the Royal Family enormously — giving them far more competence and influence than they possess. These people, who can't even manage their own family drama without it becoming global entertainment, are secretly coordinating with other reptilian bloodlines to control

world affairs would be flattering to them if it weren't so
completely divorced from reality.

What They Believe

Celebrity reptilian spotting enthusiasts claim that Hollywood actors, musicians, politicians, and other public figures are shape-shifting reptilian beings who occasionally reveal their true nature through momentary lapses in their human disguises. Believers create detailed guides for identifying these supposed "tells," analyzing red carpet photos, live performances, and television appearances with the intensity of wildlife biologists studying exotic species behavior patterns.

The supposed evidence includes vertical pupil slits caught in photographs, unusual blinking patterns during interviews, skin texture appearing scaly under certain lighting conditions, and behavioral quirks interpreted as non-human psychology. Believers claim that high-definition cameras and live streaming make it harder for reptilians to maintain perfect disguises, leading to more frequent "glitches" where their true nature becomes briefly visible.

Popular targets include politicians like Hillary Clinton, Barack Obama, and various world leaders, entertainers like Madonna, Justin Bieber, and Lady Gaga, and business leaders like Mark Zuckerberg and Jeff Bezos. Believers create extensive catalogs of supposed reptilian celebrities, often supporting their claims with screenshot compilations showing unflattering photos or unusual expressions interpreted as evidence of alien nature.

The conspiracy extends to claims that the entertainment industry is designed to showcase reptilian beings, with Hollywood serving as a recruitment center for shape-shifters who use their platforms to influence human behavior, promote reptilian agendas, and harvest emotional energy from audiences. Some versions suggest that certain musical performances, award shows, and movie premieres are reptilian rituals disguised as entertainment events.

Why It's Asinine

The supposed "evidence" for celebrity reptilian features is explained entirely by normal photographic and video artifacts: camera compression, unusual lighting, motion blur, digital noise, and the simple fact that high-definition cameras can make anyone look inhuman under the wrong conditions. Believers are analyzing technical glitches and calling them proof of alien infiltration.

The selective application of this theory is revealing, as believers tend to identify celebrities and politicians they already dislike as reptilians while ignoring similar photographic "evidence" for people they support. It's a perfect example of confirmation bias in action: the conclusion (this person is evil/alien) determines the evidence (unflattering photos prove they're reptilians) instead of evidence leading to conclusions.

The logistics of maintaining perfect disguises while performing in front of live audiences, multiple cameras, and millions of viewers makes this conspiracy impossible. Professional entertainers and politicians are some of the most scrutinized people on Earth, with every public appearance recorded and analyzed by fans, critics, and media outlets. If they were really shape-shifting reptilians, someone would have captured definitive evidence by now.

If reptilians really controlled the entertainment industry, they're remarkably bad at using it for their supposed goals. Hollywood produces movies criticizing government corruption, exposing corporate wrongdoing, and promoting individual freedom, which seems counterproductive if the goal is maintaining reptilian control over human society.

My Commentary

Celebrity lizard spotting might be the most entertaining conspiracy theory ever invented, because it combines paranoia about fame and power with wildlife photography techniques applied to red carpet events. These believers have turned celebrity watching into an amateur zoology expedition, except they're hunting for interdimensional beings instead of rare birds.

The photo analysis here is spectacular in its creativity and confirmation bias. Believers will examine hundreds of celebrity photos until they find one where lighting, camera angle, or digital compression creates an unusual effect, then declare it proof of reptilian nature while ignoring thousands of normal photos of the same person. It's like winning the lottery of selective evidence gathering.

The cultural implications are fascinating too, because this conspiracy allows people to express their discomfort with celebrity culture and political power through the lens of literal dehumanization. Don't like a politician's policies? They're not just wrong, they're a different species. Uncomfortable with celebrity influence? They're aliens manipulating you through entertainment.

Same fatal flaw as the standard reptilian theory: it requires believing that beings advanced enough to maintain perfect disguises and control global entertainment somehow can't figure out how to avoid looking weird in paparazzi photos or live television broadcasts. Either we're dealing with the most technologically advanced but cosmetically incompetent aliens in the universe, or maybe, just maybe, celebrities look strange sometimes because cameras catch people at unflattering moments and high-definition video makes everyone look slightly inhuman under the wrong conditions.

Believers have turned this into a systematic spotting guide, complete with identification criteria and evidence standards, shows how conspiracy thinking can evolve into its own form of entertainment completely disconnected from reality but internally consistent enough to feel legitimate to people who want to believe it.

Chapter 5: Space Conspiracies

Chapter Introduction

Outer space, it turns out, is not just the final frontier. It's also the final repository for beliefs that have run out of room on Earth. This chapter covers people who think the moon landing was filmed on a Hollywood soundstage, that Mars has slave colonies, and that the Sun is cold.

We're diving into four spectacular examples of people who reject everything we know about space: Moon landing deniers (Apollo 11 was filmed on a Hollywood soundstage), Mars slave colony believers (red planet labor camps run by elite pedophiles), alien abduction enthusiasts (extraterrestrials are really bad at keeping their medical experiments secret), and people who think the Sun is cold (nuclear fusion is just government propaganda).

These beliefs aren't just detached from basic physics and astronomy. They require believing that thousands of scientists, engineers, astronauts, and government officials across multiple countries and decades have maintained perfect secrecy about faking humanity's greatest achievements while somehow never producing a single credible whistleblower or piece of evidence. These folks have convinced themselves that looking through telescopes and understanding orbital mechanics is less reliable than watching grainy YouTube videos made by people who think gravity is optional.

The psychology involves anti-authority sentiment, the need to feel special for seeing “the truth,” and the comforting delusion that complex scientific achievements are elaborate deceptions anyone

can uncover with enough suspicion and free time.
Houston, we have a problem.

What They Believe

Moon landing conspiracy theorists claim the Apollo missions were elaborate hoaxes staged by NASA and the US government to win the Space Race against the Soviet Union. According to believers, no human has ever set foot on the Moon, and the famous footage of Neil Armstrong and Buzz Aldrin was filmed on movie sets, complete with special effects, carefully controlled lighting, and actors in spacesuits pretending to bounce around in low gravity.

Believers point to supposed "evidence" in the Apollo footage: the American flag appearing to wave in the airless lunar environment, the absence of stars in the lunar sky, multiple light sources creating shadows in different directions, and the pristine condition of the lunar module despite landing in a dusty environment. They claim the technology to reach the Moon didn't exist in 1969, that the Van Allen radiation belts would have killed the astronauts, and that the multiple successful missions were statistically impossible given the complexity involved.

The conspiracy supposedly involved Stanley Kubrick directing the fake Moon landing footage, using techniques he developed for "2001: A Space Odyssey." Some versions claim NASA killed Kubrick to silence him, while others suggest he left hidden clues in "The Shining" confessing to his involvement in the hoax. The motivation was to justify the massive Apollo program budget, demonstrate American technological superiority, and distract the public from the Vietnam War.

Modern moon hoax believers extend their skepticism to all space exploration, claiming the International Space Station is fake, Mars rovers are driving around in remote desert locations, and satellite imagery is computer-generated. They argue that space travel is physically impossible and that all space agencies worldwide are participating in the same elaborate deception for reasons remaining conveniently vague.

Why It's Asinine

The supposed "evidence" for a moon landing hoax demonstrates a spectacular ignorance of basic physics and photography. The flag appears to wave because it's held rigid by a horizontal support rod, and the astronauts are moving it while planting it in the lunar soil. There are no stars visible because the lunar surface is brightly lit, and the camera exposure settings necessary to film the astronauts would make stars invisible, just like how you can't see stars in daytime photos on Earth.

The shadows point in different directions because the lunar surface isn't perfectly flat, and light reflecting off the lunar module and astronauts' white spacesuits creates multiple light sources. The lunar module looks pristine because the Moon has no atmosphere to create dust storms, and the exhaust from the descent engine dispersed the surface dust instead of kicking it up like it would in an atmosphere.

The technology to reach the Moon existed in 1969. The Saturn V rocket was thoroughly tested through multiple unmanned launches, and the physics of orbital mechanics were well understood. The Van Allen radiation belts are dangerous for prolonged exposure, but the Apollo spacecraft passed through them quickly, and the astronauts received radiation doses comparable to medical X-rays, not lethal amounts.

The Soviet Union, America's primary rival in the Space Race, tracked the Apollo missions with their own equipment and confirmed their authenticity. If the moon landings were fake, the Soviets would have been the first to expose the hoax instead of quietly acknowledging American achievement. They had every motivation to debunk fake moon landings and no reason to participate in an American propaganda victory.

We have independent verification of the moon landings from multiple sources: retroreflectors left on the lunar surface by Apollo astronauts are still used today for laser ranging experiments, lunar samples brought back by the missions have been studied by scientists worldwide and show characteristics impossible to fake, and recent lunar orbiter missions have photographed the Apollo landing sites, showing the equipment left behind by the astronauts.

My Commentary

The moon landing hoax conspiracy might be the most depressing example of human achievement being met with paranoid suspicion instead of wonder and pride. These people look at one of humanity's greatest accomplishments and immediately assume it must be fake because apparently it's easier to believe in elaborate government theater than accept that engineers and scientists can do remarkable things when given sufficient resources and motivation.

The selective skepticism here is amazing. Moon hoax believers will accept that Hollywood could create convincing fake moon footage in 1969 (when special effects consisted mainly of miniatures and basic optical tricks) but refuse to believe that rocket scientists could build rockets capable of reaching the Moon. They think Stanley Kubrick could perfectly simulate lunar physics and lighting but NASA couldn't figure out how to leave Earth's orbit.

The logistics of faking the moon landings would have been more difficult than going to the Moon. You'd need thousands of people involved in the hoax: astronauts, engineers, technicians, contractors, and government officials, all maintaining perfect secrecy for over fifty years. Meanwhile, the real moon landings involved the same number of people but accomplished something historically significant instead of just lying about it.

What actually gets lost here is the thing that deserved pure human pride. This conspiracy thinking diminishes one of humanity's most inspiring achievements. The moon landings represented international cooperation, scientific advancement, and human determination to explore beyond our home planet. Moon hoax believers have turned this triumph into evidence of government deception, like looking at the pyramids and concluding they must be fake because ancient people couldn't have built them.

What They Believe

Mars slave colony conspiracy theorists claim that secret space programs have established hidden bases on Mars populated by kidnapped humans forced to work as slaves for elite controllers on Earth. According to believers, advanced spacecraft technology has been suppressed from the public while being used to transport abducted children and adults to Mars mining operations, manufacturing facilities, and research installations operated by shadowy government agencies, corporations, or alien collaborators.

The supposed slave colonies are described as underground facilities where kidnapped humans are forced to extract resources, conduct scientific experiments, or serve as breeding stock for genetic manipulation programs. Some versions claim the slaves are children chosen for their psychological malleability and physical adaptability to Mars conditions. Others suggest adults are memory-wiped and transported to Mars without their knowledge, explaining missing persons cases and unexplained disappearances.

Believers point to supposed evidence: statements by alleged whistleblowers claiming to have worked in secret space programs, unexplained NASA budget allocations supposedly funding covert Mars missions, and testimony from people claiming to have been abducted and forced to work on Mars before being returned to Earth with suppressed memories.

The conspiracy often incorporates other theories involving alien technology, time travel, interdimensional transportation, and advanced civilizations established on Mars requiring human labor for their operations. Some versions suggest the Mars colonies are preparation for elite escape from Earth during planned disasters or population reduction events.

Why It's Asinine

The practical problems with secret Mars colonies are so enormous they make every other conspiracy theory look logical by comparison. Getting to Mars requires approximately nine months of space travel using current technology, massive amounts of fuel, sophisticated life support systems, and landing capabilities that NASA is still developing for future missions. Secret programs have been routinely transporting humans to Mars while public space agencies struggle to land small rovers is logistically impossible.

Establishing sustainable human settlements on Mars would require massive infrastructure: pressurized habitats, life support systems, food production facilities, power generation, manufacturing capabilities, and constant supply runs from Earth. The cost would be astronomical, requiring resources far exceeding the budgets of entire nations, let alone secret programs supposedly operating without oversight or public funding sources.

Mars is extraordinarily hostile to human life. The atmosphere is 95% carbon dioxide with virtually no oxygen, surface pressure less than 1% of Earth's, temperatures averaging minus 80 degrees Fahrenheit, and deadly radiation exposure due to the lack of magnetic field protection. Keeping humans alive on Mars requires technology we're still developing, not something secretly implemented decades ago.

The supposed "whistleblowers" making these claims provide no verifiable evidence, documentation, or physical proof of their involvement in secret space programs. Their stories contain basic scientific errors about Mars conditions, space travel requirements, and technological capabilities revealing ignorance instead of insider knowledge.

If governments possessed the technology for routine Mars travel, they would use it for obvious strategic and economic advantages instead of hiding it for slave colonies. Mars contains valuable resources exploitable openly for enormous profit, and demonstrating superior space technology would provide tremendous political and military advantages over rival nations.

My Commentary

The Mars slave colony conspiracy represents the perfect storm of scientific illiteracy, paranoid thinking, and failure to understand the basic logistics of space travel. These people think it's easier to secretly transport kidnapped humans to another planet than to exploit them right here on Earth where transportation costs don't include nine-month space voyages and building life support systems on a frozen desert.

The economics alone should debunk this nonsense. Why would anyone spend trillions of dollars transporting slaves to Mars when human trafficking and forced labor already exist on Earth with much lower overhead costs? If you want to exploit people for labor, you don't need to build rocket ships and terraform alien worlds when there are plenty of vulnerable populations available on the planet where oxygen is free.

The technology claims are especially hilarious. These believers think secret programs have solved problems that NASA's best engineers are still working on, but somehow these technological breakthroughs never benefit humanity in any visible way. They've mastered interplanetary transportation but can't be bothered to revolutionize Earth-based travel or energy production with their advanced capabilities.

The economics alone should finish this theory. It requires believing that the most complex and expensive undertaking in human history (establishing sustainable colonies on another planet) is being used for the most economically inefficient purpose imaginable (slave labor obtainable much more cheaply on Earth). It's like believing someone invented faster-than-light travel just to make pizza deliveries slightly quicker.

What They Believe

Alien abduction believers claim that extraterrestrial beings regularly kidnap humans for medical experiments, genetic sampling, and scientific study before returning them to Earth with suppressed or fragmented memories of their experiences. According to abductees, these encounters typically involve being taken aboard spacecraft by gray-skinned aliens with large black eyes who conduct invasive medical procedures, implant tracking devices, and sometimes extract genetic material for hybrid breeding programs.

The supposed abduction experience follows remarkably consistent patterns: victims report being paralyzed in bed or while driving, seeing bright lights, losing time, and finding themselves on examination tables surrounded by alien beings. They describe medical procedures involving probes, needles, and scanning devices, communication through telepathy instead of speech, and warnings about environmental destruction or nuclear war that humans must address.

Believers claim that millions of people have been abducted but most have suppressed memories recoverable only through hypnotic regression therapy. They point to physical evidence: unexplained scars, implants allegedly showing up on medical scans, and missing time periods unexplainable through normal means.

The phenomenon often includes claims about alien-human hybrid children that abductees are shown during repeat abductions, multi-generational family abduction patterns suggesting genetic experimentation across bloodlines, and government cover-ups of alien contact to prevent panic and maintain control over advanced extraterrestrial technology.

Why It's Asinine

The remarkable consistency of abduction accounts argues against their authenticity instead of supporting it. When thousands of people report nearly identical experiences involving the same alien appearance, procedures, and spacecraft interiors, it suggests cultural contamination and shared mythology instead of independent encounters with the same extraterrestrial species. Real encounters with alien beings would likely show much more variation in appearance, technology, and behavior.

The supposed physical evidence consistently fails to withstand scientific examination. Alleged alien implants turn out to be common materials like glass fragments, metal shards, or biological tissue entering the body through normal means. Scars and marks attributed to alien procedures are explained by medical conditions, self-inflicted injuries, or normal healing processes that abductees misremember or misinterpret.

Sleep paralysis, a well-documented medical condition, explains many classic abduction symptoms: temporary paralysis upon waking, hallucinations of intruders in the bedroom, feelings of being watched or touched, and the sensation of being moved or floating. These experiences feel completely real to the person experiencing them but are neurological phenomena instead of alien encounters.

Hypnotic regression, the primary method used to "recover" abduction memories, creates false memories instead of uncovering suppressed ones. Hypnosis makes people highly suggestible and prone to incorporating suggestions from the hypnotist into their recalled "memories." The dramatic increase in abduction reports following popular movies and books about alien encounters shows how cultural influences shape these supposed memories.

If aliens were conducting ongoing medical experiments on millions of humans, they're remarkably bad at covering their tracks while simultaneously being advanced enough to travel between stars. Beings capable of interstellar travel needing to conduct crude medical procedures on unwilling subjects ignores their likely technological sophistication and scientific capabilities.

My Commentary

The alien abduction phenomenon might be the most fascinating example of how human psychology can create elaborate false memories feeling completely real to the people experiencing them. These aren't people making up stories for attention, they genuinely believe they've been kidnapped by aliens, which makes their experiences both compelling and tragic.

The cultural consistency of abduction reports reveals how powerfully media influences shape our subconscious minds. Before movies and books established the "gray alien" archetype, abduction reports described wildly different alien appearances. Once the cultural template was established, suddenly everyone was being abducted by the same species of large-eyed, gray-skinned beings. Either aliens started standardizing their appearance, or people's brains started standardizing their hallucinations.

The tragedy is that many abductees are dealing with real trauma (childhood abuse, PTSD, sleep disorders, or other psychological issues) but instead of getting appropriate treatment, they're encouraged to believe their problems stem from alien medical experiments. It's like treating depression with UFO mythology instead of mental health care.

What actually disappears in all this is the interesting question. The alien abduction narrative reduces the genuinely intriguing question of extraterrestrial life to crude medical experiments and reproductive procedures. If advanced aliens were really visiting Earth, wouldn't they have more sophisticated methods of studying us than kidnapping random people for invasive medical procedures? The whole scenario makes aliens seem less like advanced beings and more like cosmic serial killers with medical degrees.

What They Believe

"Cold Sun" theorists claim the Sun is not a massive nuclear fusion reactor generating heat and light, but a cold, electromagnetic phenomenon only appearing hot due to atmospheric effects or mysterious energy interactions. According to believers, the Sun's surface temperature is freezing, and the heat we experience on Earth is generated through other mechanisms: electromagnetic radiation interacting with our atmosphere, the Earth's core providing warmth, or unknown energy fields creating the illusion of solar heating.

Proponents argue that space is cold, astronauts report cold temperatures in space despite being closer to the Sun, and that sunlight in high altitudes or mountains feels cold instead of warm. They claim traditional solar theory is government propaganda designed to hide free energy technologies, suppress alternative physics, or maintain scientific orthodoxy benefiting certain industries.

Some versions incorporate flat Earth theories, claiming the Sun is a small, local light source only a few thousand miles above Earth instead of a massive star 93 million miles away. Others suggest the Sun is a portal, hologram, or artificial light source created by advanced civilizations or secret technology projects.

The conspiracy extends to claims that solar panels don't convert heat into electricity but tap into hidden electromagnetic or "zero-point" energy fields that scientists refuse to acknowledge. Believers argue that understanding the Sun's true nature would revolutionize energy production and eliminate humanity's dependence on fossil fuels, explaining why the truth is supposedly suppressed.

Why It's Asinine

The Sun being a nuclear fusion reactor is not a theory or belief, it's a well-established scientific fact supported by multiple independent lines of evidence. We can measure the Sun's surface temperature using spectroscopy, showing it's approximately 5,778 Kelvin (about 10,000 degrees Fahrenheit). The Sun's energy output, nuclear reactions, and physical properties have been studied extensively and match theoretical predictions about stellar physics.

Space feels cold to astronauts because heat transfer in vacuum occurs only through radiation, not conduction or convection. The Sun heats objects in space through electromagnetic radiation, but without an atmosphere to trap and circulate that heat, objects in shadow quickly radiate their heat away and become very cold. This is basic thermodynamics, not evidence that the Sun is cold.

High altitudes feel cold despite being closer to the Sun because Earth's atmosphere becomes thinner with altitude, providing fewer air molecules to absorb and retain solar energy. Mountains are cold because of atmospheric pressure and density effects, not because proximity to the Sun reveals its "true" cold nature. The temperature gradient in Earth's atmosphere is well understood and completely consistent with solar heating.

Solar panels work by converting light photons into electrical energy through the photovoltaic effect, not by harvesting heat or mysterious energy fields. The physics of solar energy conversion is well understood, demonstrated in countless experiments, and used in technologies ranging from calculator batteries to massive power plants generating electricity for entire cities.

If the Sun were cold, Earth would be a frozen rock with no liquid water, no atmosphere, and no life. The energy budget calculations for Earth's climate system depend entirely on solar input, and removing that energy source would make our planet uninhabitable within days. We're alive and discussing this proves the Sun is hot.

My Commentary

The "cold Sun" theory might be the most scientifically illiterate belief in this entire book, because it requires rejecting not just astronomy and physics, but basic observation and common sense. These people experience sunshine warming their skin and somehow conclude that the source of that warmth must be cold, like getting burned by a stove and deciding fire must be freezing.

The mental gymnastics required to maintain this belief are Olympic-level impressive. When confronted with the obvious fact that sunlight creates heat, believers invent increasingly elaborate explanations involving mysterious energy fields, atmospheric interactions, and hidden physics somehow escaping the notice of every scientist who's ever studied thermodynamics, astronomy, or basic energy transfer.

The conspiracy angle is rich because it requires believing that every physicist, astronomer, and engineer who's ever studied the Sun is either too stupid to realize it's cold or part of a massive cover-up to hide free energy technology. Meanwhile, the people who figured out the Sun's "true" nature are posting their discoveries on YouTube instead of collecting Nobel Prizes for revolutionizing our understanding of stellar physics.

Here's the simplest test: this belief system requires thinking that nuclear fusion (a process we can recreate in laboratories and observe in stars throughout the universe) is somehow fake, while the alternative explanation involving mysterious cold electromagnetic phenomena violating known physics is obviously true. It's like rejecting fire as an explanation for why stoves are hot and insisting they must be powered by invisible ice crystals creating reverse-cold energy.

People can look directly at the source of all energy on Earth and conclude it must be cold shows how conspiracy thinking can override even the most basic sensory evidence. These folks have convinced themselves that up is down, hot is cold, and the most obvious facts about our solar system are elaborate lies, which would be impressive if it weren't so tragically disconnected from reality.

Chapter 6: Time Travel and Parallel Universes

Chapter Introduction

The multiverse is a legitimate concept in theoretical physics. It is also the greatest gift the internet ever gave to people who don't want to accept that their memories are imperfect and their problems are their own fault. This chapter covers time travelers, Mandela Effect devotees, and people who think they can solve their lives by meditating into a better dimension.

We're diving into three spectacular examples of people who refuse to accept that time moves in one direction and memory is imperfect: John Titor believers (a time traveler from 2036 posted detailed predictions on early internet forums), Mandela Effect enthusiasts (misremembering things proves you've shifted between parallel universes), and quantum jumping practitioners (you can consciously move your awareness to better versions of reality where you're successful and attractive).

These beliefs aren't just detached from basic physics and neuroscience. They require believing that time, space, and consciousness work completely differently than every scientific observation suggests. But somehow they leave convenient evidence in the form of internet posts, childhood cartoon memories, and guided meditation techniques that anyone can learn on YouTube. These folks have convinced themselves that accepting personal responsibility is less appealing than believing they're interdimensional travelers whose problems stem from being stuck in the wrong reality.

Behind all this lies wishful thinking, the refusal to accept imperfect memory, and the appealing fantasy that somewhere in the multiverse there's a version of you that made better choices and is living your dream life. If you already know how this chapter ends, you've shifted timelines. Everyone else, read on.

What They Believe

John Titor believers claim a time traveler from the year 2036 posted detailed messages on internet forums in late 2000 and early 2001, warning about future events and explaining the mechanics of time travel. According to believers, Titor was a soldier sent back to 1975 to retrieve an IBM 5100 computer needed to debug legacy software in his timeline, but made a stop in our era to warn humanity about an impending American civil war beginning in 2005 and a devastating nuclear exchange in 2015.

Titor described his time machine as a C204 Gravity Distortion Time Displacement Unit manufactured by General Electric, capable of traveling through time by creating rotating black holes that bend spacetime. He provided technical diagrams, operational manuals, and detailed explanations of the physics involved, claiming his device could transport him and a small vehicle through time while requiring massive amounts of energy and creating dangerous temporal distortions.

Believers point to Titor's supposedly accurate predictions about future technology, including the development of wireless internet, the popularity of video sharing, and social media platforms that didn't exist in 2000. They claim his warnings about civil war and government overreach are coming true through political polarization, surveillance programs, and social unrest, proving his legitimacy as a genuine time traveler.

The story includes elements that believers find compelling: Titor's reluctance to reveal too much about the future to avoid paradoxes, his description of a devastated timeline where billions died in nuclear war, and his mission to save his timeline by retrieving specific technology from the past. Some believers think Titor's visit changed our timeline, explaining why his specific predictions didn't come true exactly as described.

Why It's Asinine

The John Titor story contains fundamental scientific errors that reveal it as creative fiction rather than genuine time travel accounts. His description of creating "rotating black holes" for time travel violates basic physics, because black holes are gravitational singularities that would destroy any matter they encounter, not convenient time portals that you can control with 1970s technology. The energy requirements for creating even microscopic black holes would exceed the output of entire power plants.

Titor's "predictions" were either obvious technological trends that anyone could extrapolate from existing developments or vague statements that can be retrofitted to almost any subsequent events. Wireless internet was already being developed in 2000, video sharing was a logical evolution of existing file sharing technology, and predicting social media platforms required no special knowledge of the future. His failed predictions vastly outnumber his supposed successes.

The timeline problems in Titor's story are immediately obvious to anyone familiar with time travel paradoxes. He claims to be from a future where nuclear war devastated the world, but travels to our timeline to retrieve technology. If he's from a different timeline than ours, how does retrieving technology from our past help his future? If he's from our timeline, why haven't his predicted events occurred as scheduled?

The supposed technical documentation provided by Titor reads like science fiction written by someone with a basic understanding of physics terminology but no actual knowledge of temporal mechanics, quantum physics, or the engineering requirements for the technology he describes. Real scientists examining his materials have found them scientifically incoherent and technically impossible.

Even better, Titor's story emerged during the early days of internet culture when anonymous posters could claim anything without verification. The timing, style, and content of his posts fit perfectly with early 2000s internet fiction rather than genuine communication from a time traveler warning humanity about its future.

My Commentary

The John Titor phenomenon perfectly captures the early internet's unique ability to turn creative fiction into believable mythology through the power of anonymous posting and willing suspension of disbelief. These believers have essentially turned a well-crafted piece of science fiction into evidence of actual time travel because it was posted on forums instead of published as a novel.

The selective acceptance of evidence here is remarkable. Believers will accept obviously fictional technical specifications for time machines while rejecting basic physics that explains why such devices are impossible. They'll treat vague predictions that didn't come true as evidence of timeline changes while ignoring the far simpler explanation that someone made up a story on the internet.

The psychological appeal is obvious: Titor's story provides both a fascinating mystery and a convenient explanation for why the world seems chaotic and unpredictable. Instead of accepting that the future is uncertain and complex events have complex causes, believers can imagine that someone from tomorrow visited yesterday to explain today. It's like having a cosmic spoiler alert that makes everything make sense.

Then there's the vacation problem. These believers think someone with access to time travel technology chose to spend their interdimensional vacation posting on primitive internet forums to warn strangers about distant future events they couldn't prevent anyway. Either time travelers have really poor judgment about how to use their incredible abilities, or maybe someone just wrote some entertaining fiction and people believed it because they wanted to.

What They Believe

Mandela Effect believers claim that widespread false memories of specific events, quotes, or details are evidence that people have shifted between parallel universes with slightly different histories. The phenomenon is named after people who distinctly remember Nelson Mandela dying in prison during the 1980s rather than becoming South Africa's president and dying in 2013, which believers interpret as proof they've shifted from a timeline where Mandela died earlier.

Common Mandela Effects include remembering "The Berenstein Bears" instead of "The Berenstain Bears," believing the Monopoly man wears a monocle, recalling "Sex and the City" as "Sex in the City," and thinking Darth Vader said "Luke, I am your father" instead of "No, I am your father." Believers claim these aren't simple memory errors but evidence that millions of people have collective memories of alternate realities they previously inhabited.

Believers point to the specificity and consistency of these false memories across large groups of people as evidence that parallel universe shifting is real. They argue that statistical clustering of identical false memories is too unlikely to be coincidental, suggesting instead that groups of people have shifted together from realities where these alternate versions were true.

The most elaborate versions incorporate quantum physics concepts, claiming that consciousness can slip between parallel dimensions through quantum tunneling effects or that reality itself is unstable and occasionally shifts, bringing groups of people along with it. Some believers think CERN's particle accelerator experiments have torn holes in spacetime, allowing people to accidentally fall through into alternate timelines.

Why It's Asinine

The Mandela Effect is explained entirely by well-understood psychological phenomena: false memory formation, confabulation, and social reinforcement of incorrect recall. Human memory is reconstructive, not reproductive. We don't store exact recordings of events but instead rebuild memories each time we recall them, introducing errors and modifications that become permanently integrated into our memory of what happened.

The supposed "evidence" of reality shifting falls apart when you examine the patterns of these false memories. They overwhelmingly involve minor details in children's entertainment, corporate logos, and movie quotes: exactly the types of information most likely to be misremembered, confused, or learned incorrectly in the first place. If people were really shifting between parallel universes, you'd expect some variation in major historical events, not just whether a cartoon bear family spells their name with an "e" or an "a."

The consistency of false memories across groups is explained by shared cultural experiences and common sources of misinformation. When millions of people hear the same incorrect version of a movie quote or see similar-looking logos, they develop similar false memories. This is basic psychology, not interdimensional travel documentation.

The quantum physics explanations for the Mandela Effect demonstrate complete misunderstanding of how quantum mechanics works. Quantum effects operate at subatomic scales and have no relevance to macroscopic phenomena like human consciousness or memory formation. Consciousness cannot "quantum tunnel" between parallel realities any more than you can quantum tunnel through your front door instead of opening it.

Even better, the Mandela Effect only seems to affect trivial pop culture details while leaving all major historical events, scientific discoveries, and technological developments completely unchanged. Apparently, parallel universe shifting is powerful enough to alter cartoon character names but not significant enough to change anything important about human history, which seems remarkably convenient for a supposedly cosmic phenomenon.

My Commentary

The Mandela Effect might be the most narcissistic delusion in this book because it requires believing that your imperfect memory is so important that reality itself must be wrong when it disagrees with what you remember. These people would literally prefer to believe they're interdimensional travelers than admit they misremembered a children's book title, which shows either incredible confidence or spectacular insecurity about their own fallibility.

The specificity of these supposed reality shifts is hilariously revealing. Apparently, universe-hopping only affects things like cartoon character names, corporate logos, and movie quotes while leaving everything else completely unchanged. It's like believing in cosmic forces that are powerful enough to alter reality but only care about correcting minor details in entertainment media and brand recognition.

Somewhere in this belief system, ordinary human forgetfulness became evidence of extraordinary cosmic phenomena. Instead of accepting that memory is imperfect and childhood recollections are often inaccurate, believers have created an elaborate mythology where being wrong about trivial details proves you're a interdimensional refugee from a parallel Earth.

This belief system prevents people from learning how memory works and developing better critical thinking skills about their own recall abilities. Instead of understanding the fascinating ways our brains construct and reconstruct memories, believers prefer to imagine they're quantum tourists whose consciousness accidentally wandered into the wrong timeline at some point and now everything is slightly off.

What They Believe

Quantum jumping practitioners claim they can consciously shift their awareness to parallel versions of themselves living in alternate realities where they've made different choices and achieved better outcomes. According to believers, infinite parallel universes exist containing every possible variation of your life, and through meditation, visualization, and specific mental techniques, you can transfer your consciousness to versions of yourself that are more successful, attractive, wealthy, or happy.

The practice typically involves relaxation techniques, guided visualizations, and detailed imagination of the desired alternative reality. Practitioners describe feeling themselves "shift" into bodies of their parallel selves, experiencing their alternate lives firsthand, and sometimes retaining memories or abilities from these other dimensions when they return to their original reality. Some claim to bring back foreign language skills, artistic abilities, or knowledge they didn't possess before jumping.

Believers point to quantum physics concepts like the many-worlds interpretation and parallel universe theories as scientific validation for their practices, claiming consciousness operates independently of physical laws and can navigate between different quantum realities. They argue that quantum jumping explains phenomena like deja vu, sudden inspiration, and dramatic personality changes as evidence of interdimensional consciousness transfer.

Advanced practitioners claim they can permanently shift to better realities by maintaining the vibrational frequency of their desired timeline, essentially replacing their current life with a more favorable version from a parallel universe. Some believe they can help others jump to better realities through group sessions, quantum healing practices, or teaching the visualization techniques required for successful interdimensional travel.

Why It's Asinine

Quantum jumping misappropriates legitimate physics terminology while demonstrating complete ignorance of how quantum mechanics works. The many-worlds interpretation is a theoretical framework for understanding quantum measurement, not a travel guide for consciousness tourism between parallel dimensions. Quantum effects occur at subatomic scales and have no relevance to macroscopic phenomena like human consciousness or life choices.

Guided meditation, visualization, and relaxation techniques can create vivid imaginary experiences that feel real to the person experiencing them. The brain is remarkably good at creating convincing false memories and sensations when given appropriate suggestions and motivation to believe.

If consciousness could really transfer between parallel selves, the logistics would be impossibly complex. How does your awareness find the specific alternate version you want among infinite possibilities? How do you avoid accidentally jumping into realities where your parallel self is worse off? Why would consciousness from different universes want to trade places, and what prevents unwanted interdimensional visitors from hijacking your life?

The claimed benefits of quantum jumping (learning new skills, gaining knowledge, becoming more successful) are achievable through normal means: education, practice, effort, and making better choices in your current reality. You can bypass personal growth and achievement by stealing accomplishments from your parallel selves? That's basically cosmic plagiarism with extra steps.

Real quantum physics has nothing to do with consciousness, meditation, or self-improvement. Quantum jumping practitioners have essentially created a new age version of daydreaming while claiming it's based on advanced science, which is like calling meditation "neural hacking" and pretending it gives you computer programming skills.

My Commentary

Quantum jumping might be the most elaborate excuse for avoiding personal responsibility ever invented, because it lets people believe they can improve their lives without effort by simply borrowing success from alternate versions of themselves. It's like cosmic cheating where instead of studying for the test, you just swap consciousness with the parallel you who did the homework.

The scientific misunderstanding here is breathtaking. These people have taken one of the most complex and counterintuitive areas of physics and turned it into a self-help technique based on wishful thinking and meditation apps. It's like claiming you can perform surgery because you understand that sharp things can cut, while completely missing everything about anatomy, medicine, and the difference between kitchen knives and scalpels.

The narcissism required to believe you can casually hop between parallel universes to upgrade your life is staggering. Apparently, the fundamental structure of reality exists primarily to provide improvement opportunities for people who don't want to put in effort in their current dimension. It's like believing the multiverse is your personal Netflix account where you can binge-watch better versions of your own life.

This belief system encourages people to fantasize about alternate realities instead of working to improve their current one. While believers are meditating about parallel selves who made better choices, they could be making those choices themselves in the universe they inhabit. It's like spending so much time imagining what you'd do if you won the lottery that you never buy a ticket, except worse because you convince yourself the daydreaming is the actual lottery.

Quantum jumping promises all the benefits of self-improvement without any of the work, which reveals its fundamental appeal: it's personal development for people who want to believe transformation can happen through imagination rather than action. Unfortunately, the only thing you can really change through consciousness alone is your awareness of how much effort actual improvement requires.

Chapter 7: Financial Fantasies

Chapter Introduction

Building wealth is boring, slow, and requires discipline over decades. This chapter is about people who have rejected that reality in favor of Nigerian princes, crypto prophecies, and the sacred belief that somewhere out there exists a secret the rich aren't telling you.

We're diving into three spectacular examples of people who refuse to accept that building wealth requires time, effort, and actual knowledge: Nigerian Prince Syndrome sufferers (people who still fall for email scams that predate social media), cryptocurrency cultists (digital gold bugs who think blockchain is magic), and get-rich-quick scheme believers (folks who are convinced that traditional investing is a scam but buying someone's course on forex trading is brilliant).

These beliefs aren't just financially dangerous. They represent a fundamental misunderstanding of how money, markets, and basic economics work. But they also come with the appealing fantasy that somewhere there's a secret shortcut to wealth that only requires you to be smart enough to recognize it. These folks have convinced themselves that financial literacy matters less than finding the right guru, system, or digital coin that will magically transform their bank account.

Behind all this lies wishful thinking, the refusal to accept that wealth building is boring and slow, and the seductive belief that if you're not getting rich quickly, you're doing it wrong. Your Nigerian prince is waiting.

What They Believe

Nigerian Prince Syndrome describes people who continue falling for advance fee fraud scams, despite these schemes being so well-known they've become internet jokes. Believers receive emails from supposed foreign royalty, government officials, or wealthy widows claiming they need help transferring millions of dollars out of their countries. In exchange for assistance (and upfront fees), victims are promised substantial percentages of these fictional fortunes.

Modern victims often convince themselves they've found "legitimate" versions of these scams, believing they can spot the "real" opportunities among the obvious fakes. They point to official-looking documents, convincing backstories, and patient correspondence from scammers as evidence that their particular prince, minister, or businessman is genuine. Some develop ongoing relationships with scammers lasting months or years, creating elaborate emotional investments in fictional characters.

Believers often rationalize their participation by claiming they're helping genuine people in distress while earning money for their assistance. They interpret requests for fees, taxes, or bribes as normal bureaucratic requirements rather than red flags, convincing themselves that legitimate international money transfers really do work this way. Some even travel to foreign countries to meet their scammers, maintaining belief even when obvious deceptions are revealed.

The most persistent victims develop conspiracy theories about why their money transfers keep getting delayed: corrupt government officials, banking complications, or international regulations that require additional fees to overcome. They interpret each new obstacle as proof the fortune exists instead of evidence they're being systematically robbed by criminals who have studied human psychology better than most therapists.

Why It's Asinine

International money transfers don't work through random email requests to strangers. Legitimate wealthy people, government officials, and business people have access to banks, lawyers, and financial institutions designed to handle large transactions. They don't need help from random people who respond to unsolicited emails, and they certainly don't pay strangers percentages of millions of dollars for essentially doing nothing.

The supposed "official documents" provided by scammers are easily forged, and the stories behind these scams are recycled templates that have been used thousands of times with minor variations. Real government officials don't conduct business through Gmail accounts, legitimate banks don't require "processing fees" paid via Western Union, and genuine legal procedures don't involve sending money to random people before receiving anything in return.

The psychological manipulation in these scams is sophisticated and targets specific vulnerabilities: greed, the desire to help others, and the fantasy of sudden wealth. Scammers deliberately target people who seem lonely, financially stressed, or unfamiliar with international business practices. They build emotional connections over time, making victims feel special and chosen rather than randomly targeted.

The logistics of the supposed scenarios don't make sense under any legitimate financial system. Why would a foreign prince need help from a stranger when any major bank would eagerly assist with legitimate multi-million-dollar transactions? Why would someone with access to vast wealth be unable to pay small fees themselves? The entire premise collapses under basic scrutiny.

Law enforcement agencies worldwide have documented these scams extensively, published detailed warnings, and prosecuted thousands of perpetrators. The patterns are well-known, the methods are documented, and the outcomes are always the same: victims lose money and never receive the promised fortunes. Yet new victims continue falling for essentially identical schemes with minor cosmetic changes.

My Commentary

Nigerian Prince Syndrome represents the triumph of wishful thinking over pattern recognition, where people who should know better convince themselves they've discovered the one legitimate opportunity hidden among thousands of obvious scams. These folks have essentially decided that their particular email from a stranger offering millions of dollars is the real deal, while everyone else's is fake.

This requires believing that legitimate international business is conducted through spam emails and wire transfers to random strangers. These victims think genuine wealthy people and government officials operate like characters in a badly written thriller, secretly moving money through elaborate schemes involving helpful strangers instead of using, you know, banks and lawyers like normal rich people.

What's maddening is how victims often double down when confronted with evidence of the scam. Instead of accepting they've been fooled, they create elaborate rationalizations about why their situation is different, why the warnings don't apply to them, or why everyone else is too cynical to recognize a real opportunity. It's like being told your house is on fire and explaining why the smoke is a good sign.

The emotional investment victims develop in these fictional relationships is heartbreaking. They're not just losing money to criminals, they're forming genuine attachments to characters who don't exist. When the scam inevitably collapses, victims lose both their money and their imaginary friend, which explains why some refuse to accept reality even when the evidence is overwhelming.

Perhaps most frustrating is how these scams prey on people's desire to help others and achieve financial security. Victims aren't necessarily greedy or stupid, they're often lonely people who want to believe they can make a difference while improving their own circumstances. The scammers exploit basic human decency and turn it into a weapon for financial exploitation.

What They Believe

Cryptocurrency cultists have elevated digital coins from speculative investments into religious experiences, complete with prophets, sacred texts, and unshakeable faith in the coming revolution. These believers claim traditional currency is a scam perpetrated by governments and banks, while cryptocurrencies represent the future of money, freedom, and human civilization. They speak of "hodling" (holding) their coins through any price volatility as a spiritual practice, viewing market crashes as temporary tests of faith instead of evidence of inherent volatility.

Believers often focus on specific cryptocurrencies with cult-like devotion, treating price predictions like prophecy and treating skeptics like heretics. Bitcoin maximalists claim their coin will eventually replace all other forms of money, while supporters of alternative coins believe they've discovered the "next Bitcoin" that will make them millionaires before everyone else catches on. They interpret any positive news as validation of their beliefs while dismissing negative developments as temporary setbacks or deliberate manipulation by traditional financial institutions.

The most fervent believers claim cryptocurrencies will solve virtually every economic and social problem: eliminating government corruption, ending poverty, providing financial services to the unbanked, and creating a new economic system based on mathematical algorithms rather than human institutions. They view blockchain technology as revolutionary innovation comparable to the invention of the internet, printing press, or wheel.

Advanced cultists develop elaborate theories about cryptocurrency adoption timelines, price targets that defy basic market mathematics, and conspiracy theories about why mainstream adoption hasn't occurred faster. They attend conferences with evangelical fervor, follow influencers with religious devotion, and organize online communities that function more like support groups for shared delusions than investment discussion forums.

Why It's Asinine

Cryptocurrencies are speculative assets, not revolutionary technologies that will remake human civilization. While blockchain has legitimate applications, most cryptocurrencies function more like digital collectibles than practical currencies. Their extreme price volatility, high transaction costs, slow processing times, and massive energy consumption make them unsuitable for most everyday financial activities that traditional money handles efficiently.

The technology underlying most cryptocurrencies isn't particularly innovative or complex. Distributed databases, cryptographic hashing, and digital signatures existed long before Bitcoin. The "revolutionary" aspect is mostly marketing, not technological breakthrough. Most blockchain applications can be accomplished more efficiently using existing database technologies without the complexity, cost, and environmental impact of cryptocurrency systems.

The supposed benefits of cryptocurrency adoption are largely theoretical and ignore practical realities of how modern economies function. Government monetary policy, banking regulations, and financial institutions exist for legitimate reasons, not just to oppress freedom-loving crypto enthusiasts. Replacing these systems with unregulated, anonymous, volatile digital tokens would create more problems than it solves.

The investment logic behind cryptocurrency speculation often resembles gambling more than financial planning. Believers frequently invest money they can't afford to lose, ignore basic portfolio diversification principles, and make financial decisions based on social media hype instead of fundamental analysis. The "hodl" mentality encourages people to maintain losing positions indefinitely instead of cutting losses or taking profits strategically.

The environmental impact of cryptocurrency mining is staggering, with some networks consuming more electricity than entire countries to maintain systems that process fewer transactions than traditional payment networks handle easily. The idea that this represents progress rather than wasteful inefficiency requires ignoring basic environmental and economic realities.

My Commentary

Cryptocurrency cults represent what happens when people mistake speculation for revolution and treat investment advice like religious doctrine. These believers have convinced themselves that buying digital tokens makes them early adopters of the future. In reality, they're participants in a massive speculative bubble driven by hype and fear of missing out.

The religious fervor surrounding cryptocurrencies is both hilarious and concerning. These people talk about blockchain like it's the second coming of Christ, treating routine price volatility like spiritual trials and viewing any criticism as persecution by the establishment. They've created an entire mythology where traditional finance is evil and cryptocurrencies are salvation, which would be touching if it weren't so financially dangerous.

What's absurd is how crypto cultists claim to oppose traditional financial manipulation while participating in markets that are far more manipulated than anything in traditional finance. They rail against bank fees while paying transaction costs that would make loan sharks blush, and they celebrate "decentralization" while following influencers who can move markets with a single tweet.

The psychological investment in cryptocurrency success goes far beyond financial returns. These believers have tied their identities to their digital wallets, making it psychologically impossible to acknowledge when they've made poor investment decisions. Instead of cutting losses or diversifying portfolios, they double down on failing positions and recruit new believers to validate their choices.

Perhaps most tragically, cryptocurrency cults prey on legitimate concerns about economic inequality and financial instability while offering solutions that make these problems worse. Instead of learning about traditional investing strategies that build wealth over time, believers chase volatile assets that are more likely to destroy their financial security than improve it.

What They Believe

Get-rich-quick scheme believers are convinced that traditional wealth-building advice (save money, invest regularly, live below your means) is a conspiracy to keep regular people poor while the elite use secret strategies to get rich fast. They believe there are hidden systems, insider techniques, and exclusive opportunities that can generate massive returns in short timeframes, if only you're smart enough to recognize them and brave enough to act.

These believers gravitate toward courses, seminars, and programs promising to teach "secret" methods for making money: forex trading systems that guarantee profits, real estate strategies that require no money down, internet businesses that generate passive income, or stock trading algorithms that beat the market consistently. They interpret successful marketing as evidence of legitimate opportunity, believing that anyone teaching these methods must be wealthy from using them personally.

Believers often develop collections of different get-rich-quick methods, jumping from forex trading to cryptocurrency mining to dropshipping to affiliate marketing as each previous scheme fails to deliver promised results. They rationalize failures as user error, bad timing, or insufficient commitment instead of recognizing patterns of systemic problems with the underlying promises.

The most persistent believers become part of multi-level marketing schemes or "business opportunities" where they recruit others to purchase the same courses, systems, or products they bought. They convince themselves they're helping others achieve financial freedom while perpetuating the same cycles of false promises that trapped them originally.

Advanced believers develop conspiracy theories about why traditional financial advice doesn't work: the stock market is rigged against small investors, banks deliberately keep people poor, or financial advisors profit by giving bad advice. They view conventional wisdom about slow wealth building as propaganda designed to prevent regular people from accessing the "real" secrets of the wealthy.

Why It's Asinine

If reliable methods for getting rich quickly existed, the people teaching them would use those methods to get rich instead of selling courses about them. Real wealth-building strategies are well-documented, widely available, and proven over decades: spend less than you earn, invest in diversified portfolios, and let compound returns work over time. These methods aren't secret because they're not particularly exciting or complicated.

The mathematics of compound returns explains why legitimate wealth building takes time. Even excellent investment returns of 10-12% annually require years or decades to generate life-changing wealth from modest starting amounts. Any system promising faster returns either involves extreme risk (gambling), illegal activity (fraud), or simply doesn't work as advertised.

The courses and systems being sold are profitable for their creators precisely because they don't work for students. If everyone who bought a forex trading course became wealthy, the markets would adapt and eliminate the supposed arbitrage opportunities. The real business model is selling hope and false confidence to people who want to believe wealth building can be easy and fast.

Most get-rich-quick schemes rely on recruiting new participants rather than generating legitimate business profits. Whether it's multi-level marketing, cryptocurrency schemes, or trading courses, the money flows from new recruits to earlier participants instead of from actual business activities that create genuine value.

The psychological appeal of these schemes lies in their promise to shortcut the patience and discipline required for legitimate wealth building. People want to believe they can skip the boring parts of financial planning and jump straight to being rich, which makes them perfect targets for anyone willing to sell that fantasy.

My Commentary

Get-rich-quick schemes represent the financial equivalent of believing in magic spells, where people convince themselves that the right incantation (course, system, or guru) will transform their bank account overnight. These believers have essentially decided that everyone who got wealthy through traditional methods was either lying or doing it wrong.

The irony is breathtaking: people who can't save $1,000 are convinced they can make $10,000 per month through secret trading strategies. They reject proven wealth-building advice as too slow while embracing systems that are virtually guaranteed to lose money faster than any traditional investment could possibly gain it. It's like refusing to learn to walk because you're holding out for teleportation.

What's despicable is how these schemes prey on people's legitimate financial stress and aspirations for better lives. Instead of addressing the real barriers to wealth building (low income, high expenses, lack of financial education), these programs offer magical thinking as a substitute for practical solutions. They're selling lottery tickets disguised as business strategies.

The recruitment aspect of many schemes is especially insidious because it turns victims into perpetrators. People who lose money on these systems often try to recoup their losses by selling the same false promises to friends and family, spreading the financial damage through their personal networks while convincing themselves they're offering opportunities instead of scams.

Perhaps most frustrating is how get-rich-quick believers often have access to legitimate information about wealth building but reject it as too boring or slow. They'll spend thousands of dollars on courses promising impossible returns while refusing to contribute to retirement accounts that would make them wealthy over time. It's like dying of thirst while refusing to drink water because you're waiting for someone to invent a magical hydration potion.

The persistence of these schemes across generations shows that human psychology hasn't evolved to handle modern financial complexity. People who wouldn't trust a stranger selling magic beans will send money to internet gurus promising to teach them secret wealth-building methods. The packaging has improved even though the underlying scam remains identical.

Chapter 8: Historical Revisionism Gone Wild

Chapter Introduction

History, apparently, is not what happened. It's what historians want you to think happened, while the real story — aliens, faked deaths, noble savages, and Napoleon's true height — sits suppressed in academic journals nobody reads. This chapter covers people who think they've done the research.

We're diving into four spectacular examples of people who refuse to accept that the past happened the way evidence suggests: Ancient Aliens enthusiasts (extraterrestrials built everything impressive because humans are too stupid), Napoleon height truthers (the French emperor was actually tall and this matters deeply), Library of Alexandria deniers (one of history's most famous destructions never actually occurred), and peaceful indigenous romanticizers (Native Americans lived in perfect harmony until Europeans ruined everything).

These beliefs aren't just historically inaccurate. They require believing that thousands of historians, archaeologists, and researchers across centuries have been systematically lying about the past, while random internet theorists have uncovered the real truth using YouTube videos and their superior pattern recognition skills. These folks have convinced themselves that accepting mainstream historical consensus makes you a sheep, while believing that aliens built the pyramids makes you a free thinker.

Behind all this lies the appealing fantasy that the past was more exciting than it was, the refusal to accept that ancient people were capable of impressive achievements without supernatural help, and the narcissistic belief that you're smart enough to see through historical "lies" that have fooled everyone else. The aliens are already inside.

Ancient Aliens Built Everything

What They Believe

Ancient alien theorists claim that extraterrestrial visitors helped early human civilizations build monuments, develop technologies, and advance their societies far beyond what primitive humans could achieve alone. According to believers, aliens visited Earth thousands of years ago and were interpreted as gods by ancient peoples, explaining the technological sophistication of structures like the pyramids, Stonehenge, and various megalithic sites around the world.

These theorists point to supposed evidence in ancient art, religious texts, and archaeological sites that they interpret as depicting spacecraft, astronauts, and advanced technology. They claim that rapid technological advances in ancient civilizations, precise astronomical knowledge, and sophisticated engineering techniques prove extraterrestrial intervention because humans couldn't possibly have figured these things out independently.

Believers often focus on pyramid construction precision, the massive stones used in ancient sites, detailed astronomical calendars created by civilizations without modern instruments, and religious artwork that supposedly depicts flying vehicles or beings in space suits. They argue that mainstream archaeology deliberately ignores or suppresses evidence of alien contact to maintain their academic authority.

The most elaborate versions suggest ongoing alien involvement in human development, claiming that extraterrestrials have been guiding human civilization for millennia and continue to monitor our progress. Some believers think aliens will return when humanity reaches sufficient technological or spiritual development, essentially treating human history as a cosmic science experiment with periodic check-ins from our extraterrestrial supervisors.

Why It's Asinine

The ancient alien theory is fundamentally racist because it assumes that non-European civilizations couldn't possibly have developed impressive technologies and monuments without supernatural help. Ancient peoples were just as intelligent as modern humans and had thousands of years to develop sophisticated engineering, astronomical, and mathematical knowledge through observation, experimentation, and gradual technological advancement.

The supposed "impossible" achievements of ancient civilizations are entirely possible using period-appropriate tools and techniques. Archaeologists and engineers have successfully demonstrated how pyramids could be built using ramps, levers, and organized labor. The precision of ancient stonework reflects skilled craftsmanship and time investment, not alien technology. Astronomical knowledge developed naturally from careful observation of celestial movements over generations.

The "evidence" cited by ancient alien theorists relies on misinterpretation of artwork, religious symbolism, and archaeological findings. Ancient religious art depicting gods, mythological creatures, or symbolic representations gets reinterpreted as literal depictions of spacecraft and astronauts. This approach ignores the cultural, religious, and artistic contexts in which these works were created.

The logistics of ancient alien intervention make no sense under any reasonable scenario. Why would advanced extraterrestrials capable of interstellar travel limit their assistance to moving stones and teaching astronomy? Why would they help build monuments but not share medical knowledge, metallurgy, or other technologies that would dramatically improve human welfare? Why would they leave no definitive evidence of their presence beyond ambiguous artwork and impressive architecture?

Modern archaeology provides detailed explanations for how ancient achievements were accomplished using available technologies and human ingenuity. We have extensive evidence of tool development, construction techniques, and gradual technological progression that explains these accomplishments without requiring extraterrestrial intervention. The ancient alien theory ignores this evidence in favor of sensationalized speculation.

My Commentary

The ancient alien theory might be the most accidentally insulting belief system ever devised, because it essentially argues that brown people couldn't possibly have been smart enough to build cool stuff without help from space aliens. These believers look at the pyramids, Mayan temples, or Easter Island statues and immediately conclude that the local populations must have needed extraterrestrial assistance, while somehow never questioning whether Europeans needed alien help to build their cathedrals.

The selective application of alien intervention is hilariously revealing. Apparently, extraterrestrials were happy to help move giant stones and align buildings with stars, but they completely forgot to mention antibiotics, electricity, or basic sanitation. These cosmic do-gooders had the technology for interstellar travel but decided humanity's most pressing need was help with construction projects and astronomical calendars.

The interpretation problem here is spectacular — believers read every piece of ancient art as alien contact evidence while ignoring the cultural and religious contexts that actually explain these depictions. A carving of a mythological god becomes a space helmet, religious symbolism becomes spacecraft, and artistic representation becomes documentary evidence. It's like future archaeologists concluding that Superman comics prove 20th-century humans could fly.

The conspiracy element adds another layer of ridiculousness. Thousands of archaeologists worldwide are supposedly covering up evidence of alien contact to protect their academic careers, because nothing threatens an archaeologist's job security like discovering the most important find in human history. These scholars would rather suppress world-changing evidence than publish papers that would make them the most famous researchers in history.

This theory prevents any real appreciation for the genuine achievements of ancient civilizations. Instead of marveling at human ingenuity, persistence, and creativity, believers prefer to credit imaginary aliens for everything impressive our ancestors accomplished. It's like watching a brilliant performance and insisting the artist must have had supernatural help because you can't imagine being that talented yourself.

What They Believe

Napoleon height revisionists claim that the famous French emperor wasn't actually short, but rather average or even tall for his era, and that his supposed diminutive stature is a myth perpetuated by British propaganda and measurement confusion. According to these believers, Napoleon's height has been systematically misrepresented in history books, popular culture, and collective memory as part of a deliberate campaign to diminish his legacy and make him seem less intimidating.

Believers point to supposed evidence that Napoleon was 5'7" (170 cm), which was average or above-average height for 18th-century French men. They claim that confusion between French and English measurement systems led to incorrect height calculations, and that British cartoonists deliberately depicted Napoleon as short to mock and demean him during their military conflicts.

These revisionists argue that the "short Napoleon" myth has been perpetuated through centuries of historical inaccuracy, becoming so embedded in popular culture that even historians continue repeating false information without properly examining the evidence. They claim this demonstrates how historical myths can become accepted fact through repetition and cultural reinforcement.

Some believers extend this to broader arguments about historical accuracy and the reliability of commonly accepted historical facts. They use Napoleon's height as an example of how mainstream historical narratives can be wrong about basic details, suggesting that if historians got something as simple as height wrong, what other historical facts might be inaccurate?

Why It's Asinine

Napoleon's height is well-documented through multiple sources, and he was not dramatically short. His autopsy recorded his height as 5'2" French feet, which converts to approximately 5'7" in modern measurements, making him average height for French men of his era but shorter than the European average. The "short Napoleon" perception comes mainly from British propaganda cartoons, not historical inaccuracy.

This entire controversy represents an enormous waste of intellectual energy over a trivial biographical detail that has no significance for understanding Napoleon's historical importance, military genius, or political impact. Whether Napoleon was 5'5" or 5'8" doesn't change anything about his conquests, legal reforms, or influence on European history.

The believers' obsession with this detail reveals more about their own psychological needs than any important historical correction. They seem desperate to defend Napoleon's physical stature as if it somehow affects his historical legacy, missing the point that his achievements speak for themselves regardless of his height.

The measurement confusion argument doesn't hold up under scrutiny. Contemporary sources, including medical examinations and descriptions by people who knew Napoleon personally, consistently describe him as shorter than average. The British propaganda explanation doesn't account for French sources that also noted his relatively small stature.

This crusade treats a minor historical footnote as if it's a major historiographical controversy, elevating personal appearance details to the level of important historical revision. It's the academic equivalent of arguing about whether Julius Caesar preferred red or blue togas while ignoring his actual political and military significance.

My Commentary

The Napoleon height controversy represents the triumph of pedantic obsession over historical perspective, where people get so fixated on defending a dead emperor's physical measurements that they lose sight of why anyone should care about Napoleon in the first place. These believers have essentially turned biographical trivia into a crusade for historical accuracy, as if Napoleon's military genius somehow depends on whether he was 5'5" or 5'7".

People can become emotionally invested in the weirdest historical details. These folks are more passionate about Napoleon's height than most people are about things that affect their lives. They've convinced themselves that correcting this supposed historical injustice is important work, instead of recognizing it as the ultimate example of missing the forest for the trees.

The leap from minor historical error to total institutional distrust doesn't hold up. Yes, some details in historical accounts are inaccurate, but that doesn't mean all historical knowledge is suspect. Using Napoleon's height as proof that historians can't be trusted is like arguing that because weather forecasts are sometimes wrong, meteorology is a fraud. It's a category error disguised as critical thinking.

The defensive quality of this belief is telling. Why do people feel the need to protect Napoleon's height as if it matters to his legacy? His achievements in military strategy, legal reform, and European politics are well-documented and significant regardless of whether he needed a step stool to reach high shelves. It's like arguing that Einstein's theories are less valid because he had messy hair.

This obsession with Napoleon's physical appearance distracts from actual historical complexities and controversies that deserve attention. While these believers debate measurement conversions, they could be learning about Napoleon's impact on nationalism, his legal reforms, or his role in ending the Holy Roman Empire. But apparently arguing about his height is more satisfying than understanding his actual historical significance.

What They Believe

Library of Alexandria preservation theorists claim that the famous ancient library wasn't destroyed in a single catastrophic fire as commonly believed, but instead declined gradually through funding cuts, political changes, and administrative neglect. According to these revisionists, the dramatic "burning of Alexandria" story is a historical myth that oversimplifies a complex institutional decline and unfairly blames specific groups for destroying invaluable ancient knowledge.

Believers argue that the library's decline began centuries before any supposed destruction events, pointing to evidence that the institution had already lost much of its prominence and collection by the time of alleged burning incidents. They claim that multiple supposed "destruction" events (attributed variously to Julius Caesar, Christian mobs, or Muslim conquerors) couldn't all be true, suggesting that historians have confused different incidents or invented dramatic narratives for pedagogical effect.

These theorists point to archaeological evidence suggesting that parts of the library complex continued operating for centuries after supposed destruction dates, and that ancient sources describing library burnings are often inconsistent, contradictory, or written long after the supposed events. They argue that the dramatic destruction narrative serves modern political and cultural agendas instead of reflecting historical reality.

Some believers extend this to broader arguments about how historical narratives are constructed and maintained. They use the Library of Alexandria as an example of how dramatic stories can overshadow complex realities, and how simplified historical narratives can persist despite contradictory evidence. They argue that the "burning" story has become so culturally embedded that it's treated as fact regardless of historical accuracy.

Why It's Asinine

The Library of Alexandria preservation theory misses the point entirely because nobody serious claims the library was destroyed in a single dramatic fire anyway. Modern historians have long understood that the library declined gradually through multiple factors over several centuries, exactly as these "revisionists" claim to have discovered. This isn't historical revisionism, it's catching up with academic consensus that already exists.

The supposed "myth-busting" these believers think they're doing has already been done by actual historians decades ago. Scholarly sources routinely explain that the library's decline was complex and gradual, involving political changes, funding problems, and shifting cultural priorities instead of single catastrophic destruction events. The believers are essentially arguing against a popularized narrative that serious historians don't support anyway.

The obsession with debunking the "burning" story ignores more interesting historical questions about how ancient knowledge was preserved, transmitted, and lost across different cultures and time periods. Whether the library burned dramatically or declined gradually doesn't change the fact that significant amounts of ancient knowledge were lost, or that understanding these preservation challenges is important for modern scholarship.

The believers' emphasis on defending ancient civilizations from blame for knowledge destruction creates false historical narratives where everyone was equally committed to preserving learning. In reality, different rulers, religious groups, and political movements had varying attitudes toward scholarship and knowledge preservation. Pretending otherwise doesn't serve historical accuracy.

This controversy treats a complex institutional history as if it's primarily about assigning blame or credit for knowledge preservation, missing the social, political, and economic factors that affected ancient centers of learning. It reduces nuanced historical analysis to simple narratives about good guys and bad guys.

My Commentary

The Library of Alexandria preservation theory perfectly demonstrates how people can feel intellectually superior while arguing for positions that mainstream historians already accept. These believers think they're brave truth-tellers exposing historical lies, when they're discovering things that scholars figured out decades ago and assuming they're the first people smart enough to question popular narratives.

The psychology here involves the satisfying feeling of debunking a dramatic story, even when the story being debunked is mostly a popular culture creation, not serious historical scholarship. These folks have confused Hollywood portrayals and simplified textbook explanations with actual historical analysis, then convinced themselves they're correcting academic mistakes by pointing out complexities that academics already understand.

What's funny is how this theory treats the gradual decline of an ancient institution as somehow less tragic or significant than dramatic destruction. Whether the

Library of Alexandria burned in a day or withered over decades, the result was still the loss of irreplaceable ancient knowledge. The mechanism of destruction is far less important than understanding what was lost and why.

The defensive quality of this belief reveals underlying assumptions about cultural and religious conflicts in ancient history. Believers seem concerned about assigning blame for knowledge destruction to specific groups, missing the point that understanding how and why knowledge gets preserved or lost is more valuable than determining who to blame for ancient library management failures.

This obsession with Alexandria's destruction narrative distracts from more important questions about knowledge preservation, the role of libraries in ancient societies, and how modern institutions can learn from historical examples. But apparently arguing about whether books burned quickly or slowly is more satisfying than understanding why libraries matter for civilization in the first place.

These believers claim to care about historical accuracy while focusing on the least important aspects of the Library's history.

What They Believe

Peaceful indigenous romanticizers claim that Native American societies lived in perfect harmony with nature and each other before European contact, existing as environmentally conscious pacifists who resolved conflicts through spiritual wisdom and community consensus. According to this view, indigenous peoples were essentially noble savages who had transcended warfare, territorial disputes, and resource competition through superior spiritual and social development.

These believers paint pre-Columbian America as an ecological paradise where hundreds of distinct tribes coexisted peacefully, practicing sustainable resource management and sophisticated democratic governance without the violence, inequality, or environmental destruction that characterizes "civilized" societies. They claim that indigenous peoples lived in balance with their environment for thousands of years until European colonization introduced concepts of private property, warfare, and ecological exploitation.

Believers often point to indigenous spiritual practices, oral traditions emphasizing harmony with nature, and examples of sophisticated agricultural and social systems as evidence of this peaceful utopia. They interpret archaeological evidence of large settlements and complex societies as proof of advanced peaceful cooperation, while downplaying or ignoring evidence of warfare, slavery, or environmental modification by indigenous groups.

The most extreme versions suggest that indigenous peoples had achieved a form of social evolution that Europeans were too primitive to understand, possessing advanced spiritual knowledge and social structures that could have prevented the environmental and social problems plaguing modern civilization if Europeans hadn't destroyed these superior cultures through genocide and cultural suppression.

Why It's Asinine

This romanticized view of indigenous peoples is historically inaccurate and ironically racist because it denies Native Americans their full humanity by portraying them as mystical beings incapable of the complete range of human behaviors including violence, competition, and environmental impact. Archaeological and historical evidence clearly shows that pre-Columbian societies engaged in warfare, territorial expansion, slavery, and significant environmental modification just like human societies everywhere.

Native American societies were complex and diverse, with different groups practicing different forms of governance, resource management, and conflict resolution. Some were peaceful, others were warlike. Some were environmentally conscious, others caused significant ecological changes. The Cahokia civilization collapsed partly due to environmental degradation, various Plains tribes fought extensively over hunting territories, and the Aztec Empire was built through military conquest and tribute extraction from subject peoples.

The archaeological record provides extensive evidence of prehistoric warfare among Native American groups: fortified settlements, mass graves showing signs of violence, weapons designed specifically for human combat, and artistic depictions of battles and warriors. Oral traditions from many tribes include stories of warfare, territorial disputes, and conflicts over resources that contradict the peaceful paradise narrative.

The "ecological wisdom" attributed to indigenous peoples often reflects survival necessities and available technologies, not superior environmental consciousness. When populations were small and technologies were limited, sustainable practices were required for survival. When populations grew or technologies advanced, many indigenous societies modified their environments extensively, sometimes unsustainably.

This romanticized view ignores the agency and complexity of indigenous peoples, reducing hundreds of distinct cultures with different values, practices, and social structures to a single idealized stereotype. It's the flip side of the "savage" stereotype, equally dehumanizing because it denies the full range of human experiences and motivations that characterized indigenous societies.

My Commentary

The peaceful indigenous people myth represents the ultimate example of noble savage romanticism, where people project their environmental and social anxieties onto an idealized version of the past that never existed. These believers have essentially turned Native Americans into mystical environmentalist superhumans who transcended basic human nature through spiritual enlightenment, which is about as realistic as believing in unicorns.

The psychological appeal is obvious: if indigenous peoples lived in perfect harmony before European contact, then all of humanity's problems can be blamed on Western civilization and capitalism instead of acknowledging that humans everywhere struggle with resource competition, territorial disputes, and environmental impacts. It's much more satisfying to believe in a lost golden age than to accept that these challenges are part of the human condition.

What's insulting is how this myth denies indigenous peoples their humanity by refusing to acknowledge that they were capable of the same range of behaviors as everyone else. Real Native Americans fought wars, competed for territory, modified their environments, and sometimes made unsustainable choices because they were human beings dealing with human problems, not mystical beings who had evolved beyond conflict and competition.

The selective use of evidence here is breathtaking. Believers will point to indigenous agricultural techniques and governance systems as proof of superior wisdom while completely ignoring archaeological evidence of warfare, the collapse of civilizations like Cahokia, or oral traditions that include extensive warfare narratives. They've created a fantasy version of indigenous history that serves their political and environmental agendas while ignoring actual indigenous experiences.

This romanticization prevents any real understanding of indigenous societies and their genuine achievements. Instead of appreciating the diverse and complex ways that different Native American groups adapted to their environments, resolved conflicts, and organized their societies, believers prefer to imagine a monolithic peaceful paradise that validates their criticisms of modern civilization.

The environmental aspect is especially problematic because it ignores how indigenous peoples managed resources and modified landscapes. Many Native American societies practiced sophisticated environmental management, but this involved active intervention and modification, not passive harmony. They used controlled burns, selective hunting, agricultural terracing, and other techniques that significantly altered ecosystems. Pretending they lived in untouched wilderness ignores their actual environmental knowledge and agency.

This myth also does a disservice to contemporary indigenous communities by creating impossible standards based on romanticized history. Modern Native Americans are expected to live up to these peaceful, environmentally perfect stereotypes while being denied recognition as real people dealing with contemporary challenges while maintaining their cultural identities and sovereignty.

Chapter 9: Weather Wars and Climate Control

Chapter Introduction

Welcome to the atmospheric asylum where people think Mother Nature needs a software update, government agencies control the weather like cosmic DJs, and every cloud in the sky is part of a sinister plot to poison your children. This chapter explores humans who have convinced themselves that meteorology is a conspiracy, atmospheric science is fake, and the people who predict tomorrow's weather are secretly controlling it with space lasers and chemical spraying operations.

We're diving into three spectacular examples of people who refuse to accept that weather just happens naturally: Chemtrail believers (commercial aircraft are crop-dusting the population with mind control chemicals), HAARP conspiracy theorists (Alaska has a weather machine that can trigger earthquakes and hurricanes), and cloud seeding paranoids (local governments are playing God with precipitation patterns to control agriculture and population).

These beliefs aren't just meteorologically absurd. They require believing that thousands of pilots, air traffic controllers, atmospheric scientists, and weather forecasters worldwide are participating in elaborate schemes to manipulate weather and poison populations, while somehow keeping these massive operations secret from everyone except YouTube researchers with really good eyesight and suspicious minds.

Behind all this lies the human inability to accept that complex systems like weather can be chaotic and unpredictable, the appealing fantasy that someone must be in control of natural disasters, and the narcissistic belief that every contrail in the sky is personally directed at your neighborhood. Don't look up.

What They Believe

Chemtrail believers claim that the visible trails left behind commercial aircraft aren't normal water vapor condensation trails (contrails), but deliberately sprayed chemical mixtures designed to manipulate weather patterns, control populations, or conduct atmospheric experiments on unwitting civilians. According to these theorists, governments and shadowy organizations use commercial aviation as a cover for massive aerial spraying programs that release aluminum, barium, strontium, and other substances into the atmosphere.

These believers point to persistent contrails that spread and linger in the sky as evidence of chemical spraying, claiming that normal contrails should dissipate quickly while chemtrails create artificial cloud cover that can last for hours. They argue that modern contrails are more persistent and widespread than those observed in previous decades, suggesting that something fundamental has changed about aircraft emissions or flight patterns.

Chemtrail theorists often claim these operations serve multiple sinister purposes: weather modification to create droughts or floods, population control through airborne toxins, atmospheric heating or cooling to accelerate climate change, or mass medication to make populations more docile and compliant. Some believers think the chemicals are designed to enhance electromagnetic signals for mind control purposes, turning the atmosphere into a giant antenna for thought manipulation.

The most elaborate versions incorporate supposed evidence like unusual weather patterns, increased rates of certain diseases, soil and water samples showing elevated metal concentrations, and government patents for atmospheric modification technologies. Believers often organize to document flight patterns, collect samples, and pressure government officials to acknowledge these supposed spraying programs.

Why It's Asinine

Contrails are well-understood atmospheric phenomena that form when hot jet exhaust containing water vapor meets cold air at high altitudes, causing immediate condensation and freezing into ice crystals. The persistence and spread of contrails depends entirely on atmospheric conditions like temperature, humidity, and wind patterns. When the air is humid and cold enough, contrails can persist for hours and spread into cirrus-like clouds, exactly as basic atmospheric physics predicts.

The supposed increase in persistent contrails over recent decades is explained by increased air traffic, more efficient jet engines that operate at higher altitudes, and more flights occurring at altitudes where contrail formation is likely. Modern jet engines also burn fuel more completely, producing more water vapor per gallon of fuel, which increases contrail formation under the right atmospheric conditions.

The logistics of conducting secret global spraying operations using commercial aviation would be impossible to conceal. You'd need cooperation from aircraft manufacturers, airlines, pilots, maintenance crews, air traffic controllers, fuel suppliers, and regulatory agencies worldwide. Chemtrail believers essentially claim that millions of aviation industry workers are participating in a global poisoning conspiracy while somehow never leaking credible evidence.

Aircraft don't have the equipment, fuel capacity, or payload space to conduct the massive spraying operations that chemtrail theorists describe. Commercial jets are designed to transport passengers and cargo efficiently, not to carry additional tanks of chemicals and spraying equipment. The fuel requirements alone would make operations economically impractical and easily detectable through fuel consumption monitoring.

The supposed health effects and environmental evidence cited by chemtrail believers are explained by normal pollution sources, industrial contamination, and the natural presence of metals in soil and water. Aluminum and barium occur naturally in the environment and are also released by industrial processes, vehicle emissions, and other human activities that don't require secret aircraft spraying programs.

My Commentary

The chemtrail conspiracy represents the perfect storm of scientific illiteracy, pattern recognition gone haywire, and the desperate human need to find villains responsible for everything bad that happens in the world. These believers have convinced themselves that water vapor is a weapon and that every airplane in the sky is participating in a massive aerial poisoning campaign designed to control their minds and bodies.

What's hilarious is how chemtrail believers think they've discovered a secret global conspiracy by looking up at the sky and noticing that sometimes airplane trails stick around longer than other times. They've taken basic atmospheric physics and turned it into evidence of population control, because apparently understanding why ice crystals form in cold air is too complicated, but uncovering a worldwide chemical spraying operation is totally obvious.

The selective paranoia here is breathtaking. These folks worry about imaginary chemicals being sprayed from aircraft while ignoring real air pollution from cars, factories, and power plants that demonstrably harm human health. They'll spend hours analyzing flight patterns and measuring contrail persistence while chain-smoking cigarettes and living next to coal plants, because theoretical chemtrails are scary but proven carcinogens are fine.

The logistics of the supposed conspiracy would be more complex than organizing a moon landing every single day. Chemtrail believers think airlines can secretly modify thousands of aircraft, train millions of workers to participate in global poisoning programs, and coordinate spraying operations across dozens of countries without anyone ever producing credible evidence or leaking documents. It's like believing that every McDonald's employee is secretly in the CIA.

This conspiracy theory distracts from real environmental and health issues that deserve attention. While chemtrail believers obsess over imaginary sky poisoning, real air pollution continues causing respiratory disease, climate change creates genuine weather disruption, and industrial contamination poses documented health risks. But apparently fighting imaginary problems is more satisfying than addressing real ones.

These believers have turned meteorology into a horror movie where the government controls the weather and every cloud is a chemical weapon, which would be entertaining if it weren't so detached from how the atmosphere works.

154

What They Believe

HAARP conspiracy theorists claim that the High-frequency Active Auroral Research Program in Alaska is a secret weather modification facility capable of triggering earthquakes, hurricanes, droughts, and other natural disasters through electromagnetic manipulation of the ionosphere. According to believers, HAARP uses powerful radio transmitters to heat sections of the upper atmosphere, creating atmospheric disturbances that can influence weather patterns worldwide and even cause tectonic activity.

These theorists point to the facility's impressive array of antennas and its official research into ionospheric heating as evidence that HAARP possesses capabilities far beyond what government agencies publicly admit. They claim that natural disasters occurring after periods of HAARP activity are too coincidental to be random, suggesting that earthquakes in Japan, hurricanes hitting the United States, and unusual weather patterns are artificially created by ionospheric manipulation.

Believers often extend HAARP's supposed capabilities to include mind control through electromagnetic frequency manipulation, claiming that the facility can broadcast signals that influence human brain activity, mood, and behavior on a global scale. Some versions suggest HAARP works in conjunction with chemtrail programs to enhance atmospheric conductivity and improve the effectiveness of electromagnetic weather modification and population control.

The most elaborate theories incorporate HAARP into broader new world order conspiracies, claiming that global elites use weather weapons to punish uncooperative nations, create economic instability through agricultural disruption, or reduce global populations through artificially triggered natural disasters. Believers often cite patents for ionospheric heating technology and unusual cloud formations as evidence of HAARP's secret activities.

Why It's Asinine

HAARP is a legitimate scientific research facility that studies the ionosphere using radio transmissions, but its capabilities are nowhere near what conspiracy theorists claim. The facility's total power output is about 3.6 megawatts, roughly equivalent to a large commercial radio station. This is insufficient to significantly heat large areas of the ionosphere, let alone influence weather patterns or trigger earthquakes hundreds or thousands of miles away.

The ionosphere exists 60-400 miles above Earth's surface, while weather occurs in the troposphere, which extends only about 7 miles up. Heating small patches of ionosphere could influence surface weather patterns? That ignores basic atmospheric physics and the enormous energy scales involved in weather systems. It's like trying to heat your house by warming the attic with a flashlight.

Earthquakes are caused by tectonic plate movements and stress accumulation in Earth's crust, not atmospheric heating. The energy required to trigger significant seismic activity would be thousands of times greater than HAARP's total output. The correlation between HAARP activity and natural disasters that believers cite represents classic post hoc reasoning, ignoring that natural disasters occur regularly regardless of what research facilities are doing.

The supposed mind control capabilities attributed to HAARP ignore how electromagnetic radiation interacts with biological systems. Radio waves at HAARP's frequencies don't penetrate the human skull effectively, and there's no scientific mechanism by which ionospheric heating could influence brain activity. The power levels and frequencies involved are completely inappropriate for biological effects.

Real atmospheric and climate research provides detailed explanations for weather patterns and natural disaster occurrence that don't require secret weather weapons. Climate scientists understand how ocean temperatures, atmospheric pressure systems, solar radiation, and other factors influence weather, while seismologists can explain earthquake patterns through plate tectonics and geological stress accumulation.

My Commentary

The HAARP conspiracy might be the most spectacular example of people taking a legitimate research facility and turning it into the weather control center from a Bond villain's secret lair. These believers have looked at some radio antennas in Alaska and concluded that scientists have built a machine capable of controlling the weather, triggering earthquakes, and manipulating human minds, because apparently atmospheric research is just a cover story for playing God with the planet.

The physics illiteracy required to believe HAARP can control weather is staggering. These folks think you can influence hurricane formation by heating the ionosphere 200 miles above Earth, which is like believing you can control ocean waves by warming the space station. The energy scales involved in weather systems are so enormous that HAARP's radio transmitters are about as relevant as a birthday candle in a hurricane.

The attribution problem is impossible to miss once you look for it: HAARP supposedly causes every natural disaster while believers conveniently ignore that earthquakes, hurricanes, and droughts were happening for millions of years before humans invented radio. Japan has been experiencing earthquakes since the islands formed, hurricanes have been hitting the Americas since long before Europeans arrived, and droughts are documented throughout human history. But somehow HAARP is responsible for continuing these ancient patterns.

The conspiracy requires believing that atmospheric scientists are secretly weather warriors conducting electromagnetic warfare while publishing boring research papers about ionospheric physics. These same researchers who can barely get funding for basic atmospheric studies are supposedly operating the most powerful weather control system in human history, because nothing says "secret weather weapon" like peer-reviewed publications about radio wave propagation.

The mind control aspect adds another layer of ridiculous science fiction to the conspiracy. Believers think radio waves bouncing off the ionosphere can somehow influence human brain activity, despite these signals being far too weak and the wrong frequency to have any biological effects. It's like believing you can perform brain surgery with a garage door opener because they both use radio waves.

This conspiracy theory wastes mental energy that could be directed toward understanding real atmospheric science and climate research. While HAARP believers obsess over imaginary weather weapons, climate scientists are studying how human activities influence weather patterns through greenhouse gas emissions, land use changes, and other documented mechanisms that don't require secret government facilities.

What They Believe

Cloud seeding conspiracy theorists claim that weather modification programs conducted by governments and private companies are far more extensive and sinister than officially acknowledged, involving secret operations to control precipitation patterns for economic, political, or population control purposes. While cloud seeding is a real technology used to enhance precipitation in some regions, believers argue that these programs are being used to create droughts, floods, and other weather disasters to benefit certain groups while harming others.

These theorists point to documented cloud seeding operations and government weather modification research as evidence that authorities possess far greater weather control capabilities than they publicly admit. They claim that natural-looking weather disasters are artificially created to destroy crops, manipulate food prices, force population migrations, or punish political opponents through targeted precipitation control.

Believers often focus on the use of silver iodide and other chemicals in cloud seeding operations, arguing that these substances are poisoning water supplies and agricultural lands while being disguised as beneficial weather modification. They claim that repeated cloud seeding over agricultural regions is designed to make soil less fertile or contaminate food supplies with heavy metals and other toxins.

The most elaborate versions incorporate cloud seeding into broader weather warfare theories, suggesting that corporations and governments engage in precipitation battles where competing interests try to steal moisture from each other's regions or direct storms toward specific targets. Some believers claim that cloud seeding technology has advanced far beyond what's publicly known, allowing precise control over where and when precipitation occurs.

Why It's Asinine

Cloud seeding is a real but limited technology that can increase precipitation from existing clouds by about 10-15% under ideal conditions, but it cannot create weather systems or control where storms develop. The technology works by introducing particles into clouds that already contain supercooled water droplets, providing additional nucleation sites for ice crystal formation. You can't seed clouds that don't exist, and you can't make rain fall where atmospheric conditions don't support precipitation.

The chemicals used in cloud seeding, primarily silver iodide, are used in extremely small quantities and pose minimal environmental or health risks when properly applied. A typical cloud seeding operation releases about as much silver into the environment as a small photography lab, and environmental monitoring studies have found no significant accumulation of these materials in soil or water supplies.

The supposed precision control over weather patterns that conspiracy theorists describe is impossible with current technology. Cloud seeding requires specific atmospheric conditions to be effective, and even then, the results are statistical increases in precipitation over large areas instead of targeted weather creation. You can't direct individual storms or create droughts in specific locations using existing cloud seeding techniques.

The economic motives attributed to secret weather modification programs don't make sense given the unpredictable and limited nature of cloud seeding results. If corporations or governments could reliably control precipitation patterns, they would use this technology openly to increase agricultural productivity and water supplies instead of conducting secret operations with uncertain outcomes.

Real weather modification research is conducted openly by meteorologists and atmospheric scientists who publish their results in peer-reviewed journals. The limitations and challenges of cloud seeding are well-documented, and researchers continue working to improve the technology's effectiveness instead of concealing advanced capabilities that don't exist.

My Commentary

The cloud seeding conspiracy represents what happens when people take a real but limited technology and imagine it's been secretly perfected into a weather control superweapon. These believers have taken the fact that scientists can slightly increase rainfall from existing clouds and concluded that government agencies are conducting precision weather warfare using silver iodide as both a weapon and a poison.

The paranoia here is fascinating because cloud seeding is one of the most openly discussed and documented forms of weather modification. Scientists publish papers about it, governments announce when they're doing it, and the results are measurable and modest. But conspiracy theorists look at this transparency and conclude it must be hiding something much more sinister, because apparently admitting you can increase rainfall by 10% is a cover story for controlling all weather everywhere.

What's hilarious is how believers imagine cloud seeding operations work like some kind of meteorological video game where operators can target specific farms, cities, or regions with surgical precision. Real cloud seeding involves flying planes into existing storm systems and hoping that slightly more rain falls somewhere in a general area, which is about as precise as trying to control where your sneeze lands by changing your breakfast cereal.

The supposed poisoning aspect reveals the classic conspiracy theory pattern of turning beneficial technologies into evil plots. Silver iodide is used in tiny quantities precisely because it's effective at ice nucleation, not because it's a poison. But conspiracy theorists have convinced themselves that weather modification programs are secretly designed to contaminate food and water supplies, because apparently scientists spent decades developing precipitation enhancement techniques as an elaborate way to sprinkle barely detectable amounts of silver on farmland.

The economic warfare theories are absurd because they assume cloud seeding is far more reliable and controllable than it is. These believers think corporations are stealing rain from each other using weather modification technology that works maybe 15% better than doing nothing under perfect conditions. It's like imagining that slot machine manufacturers are conducting economic warfare by making their machines slightly more likely to pay out.

This conspiracy prevents any real understanding of weather modification research and its genuine limitations. While believers obsess over imaginary weather control operations, atmospheric scientists continue struggling with the basic challenges of making cloud seeding more effective and reliable. The gap between what conspiracy theorists think weather modification can do and what it can do is wider than the gap between fantasy and reality.

Chapter 10: Internet Echo Chambers

Chapter Introduction

Before the internet, a person who believed that Hollywood celebrities harvest children's blood for a rejuvenating chemical would have been alone with that belief. This chapter covers what happened when those people found each other.

We're diving into three spectacular examples of how social media and online communities can transform normal human stupidity into weaponized collective insanity: QAnon believers (a 4chan troll convinced millions that Hollywood celebrities eat children), Pizza Gate investigators (people who turned a pizza restaurant into the headquarters of an imaginary pedophile ring), and Birds Aren't Real followers (who may or may not be serious about government spy drones replacing all birds).

These beliefs aren't just disconnected from reality. They represent the internet's unique ability to take fringe conspiracy theories and turn them into mass movements through algorithmic amplification, social proof, and the human tendency to mistake Google searches for research. These folks have convinced themselves that spending hours in Facebook groups and YouTube rabbit holes makes them investigators, while dismissing journalism and evidence as "mainstream media lies."

Behind all this lies the intoxicating feeling of having secret knowledge, the comfort of finding communities that validate your wildest suspicions, and the addictive dopamine hit of connecting random dots into elaborate patterns that make you feel like the smartest person in the room. The comments section awaits.

What They Believe

QAnon followers believe that an anonymous internet poster called "Q" is a high-level government insider with access to classified information about a secret war between Donald Trump and a global cabal of Satan-worshipping pedophiles who control world governments, financial systems, and entertainment industries. According to believers, this cabal harvests adrenochrome from children's blood to maintain their youth and power, while Trump and military allies work to expose and destroy this network.

The conspiracy centers around "Q drops," cryptic messages posted on anonymous imageboards that believers interpret as coded communications about ongoing operations against the deep state. Followers spend countless hours analyzing these posts for hidden meanings, dates, and predictions about when major arrests and revelations will occur. They call this process "doing research," though it primarily involves finding patterns in intentionally vague statements and connecting unrelated events.

QAnon believers claim that mainstream media, social media platforms, and government agencies are controlled by the cabal and suppress information about their activities. They interpret any criticism or fact-checking of their theories as evidence of the conspiracy's power and desperation. When predictions fail to materialize, believers adjust their timelines or claim that disinformation was necessary to confuse the enemy.

The movement has evolved to incorporate virtually every existing conspiracy theory, from anti-vaccine beliefs to election fraud claims to COVID-19 misinformation. Believers often describe experiencing a "Great Awakening" where they suddenly understand the "truth" about world events, leading them to evangelize friends and family members who they believe are still "asleep" and controlled by mainstream media propaganda.

Why It's Asinine

QAnon originated from anonymous posts on 4chan, an imageboard known for trolling, pranks, and deliberately spreading false information for entertainment. The "Q" persona has all the hallmarks of an elaborate troll operation designed to see how many people would believe increasingly absurd claims presented with the authority of insider knowledge. The posts contain no verifiable information and make predictions that consistently fail to occur.

The supposed evidence for QAnon claims consists entirely of coincidences, misinterpreted symbols, and connections that exist only in the minds of believers who are determined to find patterns regardless of their significance. The movement relies on confirmation bias, where any event can be interpreted as supporting the conspiracy while contradictory evidence is dismissed as disinformation or part of the cover-up.

The logistics of the supposed global conspiracy would require coordination between millions of people across different countries, cultures, political systems, and time periods. Hollywood celebrities, world leaders, business executives, and other elites are all participating in elaborate Satanic rituals while maintaining perfect secrecy? That defies basic understanding of how human organizations and information security work.

The adrenochrome claims are medically nonsensical. Adrenochrome is a real chemical compound that can be synthesized in laboratories and has no youth-preserving properties. The conspiracy theory appears to be based on fictional portrayals in movies and books instead of any scientific or medical reality about how the compound works or what it does in the human body.

Law enforcement agencies have investigated claims related to QAnon theories and found no evidence of the massive criminal networks described by believers. Instead, QAnon-motivated people have committed real crimes while pursuing imaginary threats, including harassment, threats, and violence against innocent people they believed were involved in conspiracies.

My Commentary

QAnon represents the ultimate triumph of internet culture over critical thinking, where anonymous trolls discovered they could convince millions of people to believe anything as long as it was presented as secret knowledge that made them feel special and informed. These believers have turned 4chan shitposting into a religious movement, complete with prophecies, sacred texts, and the unshakeable faith that their anonymous prophet will eventually be proven right about everything.

QAnon demonstrates how people can mistake pattern recognition for intelligence and obsessive dot-connecting for research. QAnon followers spend hours analyzing random posts for hidden meanings and call it investigation, while dismissing journalism that involves source verification, fact-checking, and accountability as "fake news." It's like believing that reading tea leaves is more reliable than reading newspapers.

What's absurd is how the movement has turned failed predictions into proof of its own validity. When mass arrests don't happen, when promised revelations never materialize, and when specific claims are debunked, believers don't question their theories. Instead, they decide that disinformation was necessary, that the timeline shifted, or that the deep state is more powerful than expected. It's like a conspiracy theory that's been vaccinated against reality.

The evangelical aspect of QAnon reveals how conspiracy theories can function like religious movements, complete with conversion experiences, missionary work, and the division of the world into believers and the "asleep." These folks genuinely believe they're saving their friends and family by sharing increasingly unhinged theories, not recognizing that they're destroying relationships while chasing phantoms created by internet trolls.

People can be convinced that Hollywood celebrities are harvesting chemicals from children based on anonymous internet posts? That shows how far removed from reality online echo chambers can become. These believers live in a world where Tom Hanks is a Satan-worshipping pedophile but random posts from "Q" represent unshakeable truth, which suggests their reality testing mechanisms have been completely broken by prolonged exposure to algorithmic confirmation bias.

This movement has caused real harm to real people while pursuing imaginary threats, turning ordinary citizens into vigilantes chasing conspiracies that exist only in their heads. It's like watching people burn down their own neighborhoods while convinced they're fighting invisible monsters, except the monsters were created by internet trolls who thought it would be funny to see how many people they could fool.

What They Believe

Pizza Gate believers claim that Comet Ping Pong, a Washington D.C. pizza restaurant, served as the headquarters for a child trafficking ring operated by prominent Democratic politicians and connected to Hillary Clinton's 2016 presidential campaign. According to this theory, restaurant owner James Alefantis was coordinating a pedophile network that used coded language in emails and social media posts to communicate about their activities.

The conspiracy theory emerged from interpretations of emails released by WikiLeaks during the 2016 election, where believers claimed that references to food items like pizza, pasta, and hot dogs were code words for various forms of child abuse. They pointed to social media posts, restaurant decor, and artwork as evidence of hidden messages and symbols related to pedophile networks, interpreting normal business communications and casual social media content as proof of criminal activity.

Believers organized online investigations to analyze every aspect of the restaurant's online presence, from Instagram photos to customer reviews, looking for hidden clues about the supposed trafficking operation. They created elaborate charts connecting the restaurant to other businesses, politicians, and public figures, building a conspiracy network based entirely on geographic proximity, social media interactions, and coincidental similarities in imagery or language.

The theory expanded to include other restaurants and businesses in the area, with believers claiming to have discovered an entire network of trafficking locations hidden in plain sight throughout Washington D.C. Some versions incorporated broader conspiracy theories about global elite pedophile rings, connecting Pizza Gate to other unrelated cases and creating a comprehensive worldview where child trafficking operations are everywhere but somehow completely invisible to law enforcement.

Why It's Asinine

The entire Pizza Gate conspiracy is based on misinterpretation of normal business communications and social media posts by people who were determined to find evidence of criminal activity regardless of what the evidence showed. The supposed "code words" in emails are explained by the simple fact that the people involved in the communications ran restaurants and catering businesses where discussing food would be normal and frequent.

Law enforcement agencies thoroughly investigated the claims and found no evidence of any criminal activity at Comet Ping Pong or related businesses. The FBI, local police, and other agencies found no evidence of child trafficking, no evidence of the supposed basement operations (the restaurant doesn't even have a basement), and no evidence of any of the criminal networks described by conspiracy theorists.

The "symbols" and "coded messages" that believers identified in restaurant decor, artwork, and social media posts are examples of pattern recognition gone haywire, where people see meaningful connections in random coincidences and normal business operations. The same analytical approach applied to any business would produce equally "suspicious" results because humans are remarkably good at finding patterns even when no meaningful patterns exist.

The conspiracy theory caused real harm to real people, including death threats against restaurant employees, harassment of customers, and ultimately an armed attack by a believer who drove to the restaurant to "investigate" the basement that doesn't exist. The person most responsible for spreading the theory later admitted that he had never visited the restaurant or conducted any investigation before promoting the conspiracy to millions of people.

The supposed evidence for Pizza Gate wouldn't meet the standards for any legitimate investigation or journalism. Believers relied on speculation, misinterpretation, and guilt by association while ignoring evidence that contradicted their theories. They created a criminal case out of thin air and then acted surprised when reality failed to conform to their fantasies.

My Commentary

Pizza Gate represents the horrifying moment when internet conspiracy theorists graduated from harmless pattern recognition to potentially deadly vigilante justice, all based on their profound misunderstanding of how email works and their inability to recognize that sometimes pizza just means pizza. These believers turned normal restaurant communications into evidence of child trafficking because they couldn't comprehend that people who run food businesses talk about food frequently.

The analytical methods used by Pizza Gate investigators would be hilarious if they weren't so dangerous. These folks examined every Instagram photo, every piece of artwork, and every casual comment with the intensity of forensic investigators, but with none of the training, objectivity, or accountability that real investigations require. They basically turned restaurant reviewing into criminal investigation, except they were looking for evidence of crimes that existed only in their imaginations.

What's breathtaking is how believers convinced themselves they had uncovered a massive criminal conspiracy that somehow escaped the notice of law enforcement agencies, professional journalists, and anyone else with investigative training or legal authority. They thought their amateur internet sleuthing was more reliable than FBI investigations, which suggests a level of narcissism that would be impressive if it weren't so destructive.

The code word obsession reveals how conspiracy thinking can transform ordinary language into sinister communications. Pizza Gate believers developed an elaborate mythology where every food reference was secretly about child abuse, which means they turned normal human conversation into evidence of criminality. By their logic, every restaurant in America is probably running a trafficking ring because people discuss food all the time.

The real tragedy is how this conspiracy theory diverted attention and energy from child protection efforts while putting innocent people in danger. While believers were harassing pizza restaurant employees based on misinterpreted emails, real trafficking victims needed help from people who understand how these crimes work and how to investigate them properly.

Someone showed up with a gun to investigate a basement that doesn't exist? That perfectly captures the danger of online conspiracy theories when they migrate to real-world action. These believers created an entirely fictional criminal enterprise, convinced themselves it was real through collective reinforcement, and then acted on their delusions in ways that threatened innocent people's lives.

What They Believe

Birds Aren't Real followers claim that the U.S. government systematically killed all birds between 1959 and 2001 and replaced them with surveillance drones designed to monitor American citizens. According to this theory, what people think are birds are sophisticated robotic devices equipped with cameras, microphones, and tracking technology that report directly to government agencies for mass surveillance purposes.

The movement's supposed founder, Peter McIndoe, claims that birds were eliminated through a coordinated poisoning campaign disguised as environmental protection efforts, and that the replacement process involved releasing billions of drone replicas that perfectly mimic bird behavior, migration patterns, and biological functions. Believers point to bird perching on power lines as evidence of recharging behavior, and they interpret bird droppings as battery acid or mechanical lubricants.

Followers organize "protests" where they hold signs with slogans like "Birds Aren't Real" and "Wake Up America," attracting attention from media outlets and genuine conspiracy theorists who don't realize they're being pranked. The movement has created elaborate backstories, fake documentation, and detailed explanations for how the bird replacement program supposedly works, maintaining the satirical conspiracy with remarkable consistency and commitment.

The theory incorporates elements of real government surveillance programs and privacy concerns, using examples of government overreach and corporate data collection to make the bird replacement conspiracy seem more plausible to people who are genuinely worried about privacy and surveillance issues.

Why It's Asinine

Birds Aren't Real is a deliberate parody of conspiracy theories created by college students to satirize the absurdity of internet-driven conspiracy movements and highlight how easily people can be convinced to believe ridiculous claims when they're presented with confidence and backed by a committed community of believers.

The movement's creator has explicitly stated that Birds Aren't Real is satirical and designed to demonstrate how conspiracy theories spread and gain followers, not to convince people that birds are government drones. The entire operation functions as performance art and social commentary about the nature of belief, misinformation, and the psychology of conspiracy thinking.

The supposed evidence for bird replacement (perching on power lines, dropping patterns, migration behavior) is easily explained by bird biology and behavior that has been observed and documented for centuries before modern surveillance technology existed. Birds perch on power lines because they provide convenient resting spots, not because they need to recharge batteries.

The logistics of replacing billions of birds with mechanical drones while maintaining perfect ecological balance and biological credibility would be technologically impossible and economically prohibitive. The engineering required to create drones that perfectly mimic bird flight, feeding behavior, reproduction, and migration would far exceed current technological capabilities and cost more than any surveillance program could justify.

Real ornithologists, wildlife biologists, and animal researchers have spent careers studying bird behavior, anatomy, and physiology, providing extensive documentation of how birds work as biological organisms instead of mechanical devices. The scientific understanding of avian biology is comprehensive and inconsistent with any mechanical replacement theory.

My Commentary

Birds Aren't Real represents either the most brilliant satirical commentary on conspiracy culture ever created or the most elaborate troll operation in internet history, and some people can't tell the difference? That perfectly illustrates how far down the rabbit hole conspiracy thinking has taken American discourse. These "believers" have created a conspiracy theory so absurd that it functions as its own debunking, yet some people still fall for it because they've lost the ability to distinguish between parody and reality.

The genius of Birds Aren't Real lies in how it exposes the mechanics of conspiracy theory development and spread while simultaneously functioning as a conspiracy theory for people who don't understand the joke. It's like watching people take The Onion seriously, except the joke is designed to reveal how conspiracy theories manipulate people's legitimate concerns about surveillance and government overreach.

What's hilarious is how the movement has attracted genuine conspiracy theorists who think they've found kindred spirits, not realizing they're being mocked by college students who understand conspiracy psychology better than they understand their own beliefs. These folks show up to "Birds Aren't Real" protests thinking they're part of a truth movement, when they're participating in street theater designed to make fun of them.

Some people genuinely believe birds are government surveillance drones? That shows how completely detached from basic biology and common sense internet conspiracy culture has become. These believers look at sparrows and think "sophisticated surveillance equipment," which suggests they've never observed how birds behave, reproduce, eat, or interact with their environment.

Birds Aren't Real also reveals how conspiracy theories can function as social bonding experiences where the truth value of the beliefs matters less than the community and identity they provide. Some participants probably know it's satirical but continue participating because they enjoy the performance aspect and the community it creates, which shows how conspiracy movements can persist even when their core claims are obviously false.

The movement perfectly captures the absurdity of living in an information environment where people will believe anything that confirms their suspicions about government surveillance while rejecting basic scientific literacy about how the natural world works. It's like a conspiracy theory designed by philosophers to illustrate how far human reasoning can drift from reality when it's untethered from empirical evidence and critical thinking.

Chapter 11: Supernatural Marketplace

Chapter Introduction

Welcome to the carnival of the credulous, where people think the afterlife operates like Yelp reviews, Bigfoot is just really good at hide-and-seek, and psychic hotlines provide better relationship advice than therapists with degrees. This chapter explores the thriving industry built around people's desire to believe in magic, mystery, and the supernatural, complete with ghost hunters who think EMF detectors are scientific instruments, cryptozoology enthusiasts who mistake blurry photos for proof of unknown species, and folks who pay premium rates to have strangers guess what their dead grandmother might have said.

We're diving into three spectacular examples of how people turn wishful thinking into expensive hobbies: Ghost hunting as science (people who think paranormal investigation involves more than just scaring themselves in dark places), Bigfoot research expeditions (cryptozoologists who have turned "I saw something big and hairy" into a legitimate field of study), and psychic hotline devotees (customers who believe strangers with fake accents can predict their futures better than weather forecasters can predict tomorrow's temperature).

These beliefs aren't just scientifically baseless. They represent entire industries built on exploiting people's fear of death, love of mystery, and desperate hope that reality is more exciting than it appears. These folks have convinced themselves that paying for ghost tours makes them researchers, that buying expensive equipment turns them into scientists, and that calling psychic hotlines counts as therapy or spiritual guidance.

Behind all this lies the human need to believe we're not alone in the universe, the desire for life to continue after death, and the comforting fantasy that someone, somewhere, has access to hidden knowledge about our futures and the mysteries of existence. The spirits are restless tonight.

The spirits are restless tonight.

Ghost Hunting as Scienc The spirits are restless tonight.

What They Believe

Ghost hunting enthusiasts claim they're conducting legitimate scientific research into paranormal phenomena using electronic equipment to detect, measure, and communicate with spirits of deceased people. These modern paranormal investigators believe that ghosts can be studied using electromagnetic field detectors, digital thermometers, voice recorders, and various other devices that supposedly respond to supernatural presence or energy.

Believers point to electronic voice phenomena (EVP), unexplained temperature fluctuations, electromagnetic field spikes, and equipment malfunctions as evidence of ghostly activity. They interpret these readings as proof that consciousness survives bodily death and that spirits can interact with the physical world through electromagnetic manipulation or energy fields that their equipment can detect and measure.

Ghost hunting groups organize investigations at supposedly haunted locations, often using structured protocols they believe constitute scientific methodology. They document their findings, share evidence online, and build databases of paranormal activity they claim demonstrate consistent patterns of supernatural behavior across different locations and time periods.

Many believers extend their ghost hunting activities into broader claims about afterlife research, spirit communication, and the nature of consciousness beyond death. Some think they're advancing human understanding of what happens after we die, while others believe they're providing comfort to grieving families by proving that their loved ones continue to exist in some form after death.

Why It's Asinine

Electronic equipment used by ghost hunters detects real electromagnetic phenomena, but these readings are caused by normal environmental factors like electrical wiring, cell phone signals, radio broadcasts, solar activity, and thermal changes, not supernatural entities. EMF detectors, thermometers, and audio recorders are designed to measure physical phenomena that have natural explanations, not paranormal activity.

The supposed evidence collected by ghost hunters fails to meet basic scientific standards for reliability, reproducibility, or peer review. EVP recordings typically consist of random background noise that investigators interpret as voices through a psychological phenomenon called pareidolia, where the brain finds patterns in ambiguous stimuli. Temperature fluctuations and equipment readings have mundane explanations related to building ventilation, electrical systems, and normal environmental variation.

Real scientific investigation requires controlled conditions, standardized protocols, statistical analysis, and independent verification, none of which characterizes ghost hunting activities. These investigations typically occur in old buildings with known electrical problems, poor ventilation, and environmental factors that easily explain the anomalous readings that believers attribute to supernatural causes.

Consciousness can survive bodily death and interact with electromagnetic equipment? That contradicts everything we understand about neuroscience, physics, and the relationship between mind and brain. There's no known mechanism by which deceased consciousness could manipulate electronic devices or create measurable electromagnetic effects.

Professional scientists have tested paranormal claims under controlled laboratory conditions for decades without finding reliable evidence for ghostly phenomena. When ghost hunting evidence is subjected to proper scientific scrutiny, supernatural explanations consistently fail while natural explanations account for all observed phenomena.

My Commentary

Ghost hunting represents the perfect example of people who want to be scientists without doing the boring parts like learning physics, understanding statistics, or accepting results that contradict their beliefs. These folks have convinced themselves that buying expensive electronic equipment makes them researchers, when what they're doing is high-tech ghost stories with scientific-sounding narration.

Ghost hunters genuinely believe they're conducting rigorous investigations while using methodology that would make a middle school science teacher weep.

What's hilarious is how ghost hunters interpret every equipment malfunction as evidence of supernatural activity while completely ignoring that their devices are often cheap consumer electronics being used in dusty, humid, electrically noisy environments where equipment problems are practically guaranteed. A camera battery dies in a cold, damp basement? Must be ghosts draining the energy, not basic physics.

The EVP phenomenon is ridiculous because believers play recordings of static and random noise, then claim to hear voices speaking specific words that somehow always relate to the location's supposed history. It's like a supernatural Rorschach test where people hear what they want to hear in audio pareidolia, except they think they're documenting conversations with dead people.

Ghost hunting shows how people can mistake entertainment for education and confuse emotional experiences with scientific discovery. These investigators get genuinely scared in dark, spooky locations and interpret their fear response as evidence of paranormal activity, not recognizing that humans are biologically programmed to feel uneasy in unfamiliar, dark environments regardless of whether any ghosts are present.

The tragedy is how ghost hunting exploits people's grief and fear of death by offering false hope that consciousness survives bodily death and that they can maintain contact with deceased loved ones. Instead of helping people process loss and accept mortality, ghost hunters sell the comforting lie that death isn't real and that paying for paranormal investigations can provide closure or ongoing relationships with the dead.

What They Believe

Bigfoot researchers, or cryptozoologists, claim that North America hosts populations of large, undiscovered primate species that have successfully avoided scientific documentation despite centuries of human settlement and exploration. These believers think Sasquatch, Yeti, and similar creatures represent relict populations of ancient hominids or unknown species that live in remote wilderness areas where they occasionally encounter humans.

Enthusiasts organize expeditions equipped with cameras, audio recording equipment, plaster casting materials, and various detection devices to search for evidence of these creatures in forests, mountains, and other wilderness areas. They analyze footprint casts, hair samples, audio recordings, and photographic evidence they believe proves the existence of unknown primate species living in North American wilderness.

Bigfoot believers often point to Native American legends, historical accounts of wild men, and the consistency of eyewitness descriptions across different regions and time periods as cultural evidence supporting the creature's existence. They argue that the similarity of reports from unconnected witnesses suggests a real animal instead of folklore or hoaxes.

Many researchers extend their investigations into broader claims about hidden species, government cover-ups, and the possibility that Bigfoot represents a more intelligent creature than assumed, possibly explaining why it has avoided capture or clear documentation. Some believe these creatures possess near-human intelligence that helps them evade detection by human investigators.

Why It's Asinine

Large primates require substantial food sources, breeding populations, and territorial ranges that would make them impossible to hide in regions with extensive human settlement, hunting, logging, and recreational activity. North America has been thoroughly explored, mapped, and developed for centuries, making the existence of breeding populations of large, unknown mammals extremely unlikely.

The supposed evidence for Bigfoot consists entirely of ambiguous footprints, blurry photographs, unclear audio recordings, and eyewitness accounts that could be explained by known animals, hoaxes, or misidentification. Despite decades of expeditions by thousands of enthusiasts with increasingly sophisticated equipment, no one has produced clear photographs, video footage, or physical remains that would constitute proof of an unknown species.

Professional wildlife biologists and zoologists have examined Bigfoot evidence and found no credible support for the existence of unknown North American primates. Hair samples submitted for analysis consistently turn out to be from known animals, DNA analysis fails to identify unknown species, and footprint analysis reveals inconsistencies and anatomical impossibilities that suggest hoaxing or misinterpretation.

The fossil record shows no evidence of large primate species in North America during the timeframes when Bigfoot encounters are supposed to have occurred. The evolutionary history and biogeography of primates make it extremely unlikely that these species could have evolved or migrated to North America without leaving extensive fossil evidence.

Scientific discovery of new large mammal species requires peer-reviewed research, museum specimens, and reproducible evidence that can be verified by independent researchers. Bigfoot research has never produced evidence that meets these basic scientific standards, instead relying on anecdotal reports and ambiguous findings that don't constitute scientific proof.

My Commentary

Bigfoot research represents the triumph of hope over zoology, where people who really want to discover new species have convinced themselves that believing hard enough can substitute for understanding how biological discovery works. These folks have turned "I saw something big and hairy in the woods" into an entire field of study, complete with expeditions, conferences, and enough specialized equipment to make real wildlife researchers jealous.

The persistence of Bigfoot belief despite the complete absence of credible evidence shows how people can maintain faith in propositions that reality consistently fails to support. These researchers have been looking for the same creature for decades using increasingly sophisticated technology, yet somehow the evidence keeps getting worse instead of better as cameras improve and wilderness areas become more accessible.

The research claim collapses immediately: Bigfoot enthusiasts think they're doing legitimate zoology while ignoring everything professional biologists know about animal behavior, population dynamics, and species discovery. They imagine that large primates can maintain breeding populations in regions crawling with hunters, hikers, and researchers without leaving behind bodies, clear photographs, or definitive physical evidence.

The supposed evidence for Bigfoot reads like a greatest hits collection of hoaxing techniques and misidentification errors. Blurry photos that could be anything, footprints that show anatomical impossibilities, audio recordings that sound like known animals or humans making noise, and hair samples that always turn out to be from bears or other mundane creatures. It's like a masterclass in how not to document wildlife.

Bigfoot research also reveals how people can mistake tourism for science and confuse wishful thinking for discovery. These expeditions are expensive camping trips where participants hope to encounter something extraordinary, but they frame their nature walks as scientific research because they bring cameras and casting materials along for the hike.

The cultural staying power of Bigfoot reflects our nostalgia for a world that still contains mysteries and unknown creatures, but these believers have confused their desire for mystery with evidence of hidden species. They want to live in a world where dragons might be real and unexplored territories still exist, so they've created a mythology where North America's forests hide undiscovered giants instead of accepting that most of the mystery has been mapped out of the modern world.

What They Believe

Psychic hotline customers believe that strangers with claimed supernatural abilities can provide insights into their futures, relationships, and life decisions through telephone conversations that often cost several dollars per minute. These callers think that psychics possess genuine clairvoyant abilities, telepathic powers, or spiritual connections that allow them to perceive information about callers' lives and futures that wouldn't be available through normal means.

Believers often develop ongoing relationships with specific psychics, calling regularly for guidance on major life decisions, relationship problems, career changes, and other personal issues. They interpret accurate statements made by psychics as proof of supernatural ability while dismissing incorrect predictions as misinterpretations or changes in their life circumstances that altered predicted outcomes.

Many customers believe that psychics can communicate with deceased relatives, provide closure on unresolved grief, or deliver messages from the afterlife that offer comfort and guidance. They think these conversations represent genuine contact with spirits who want to help them navigate life challenges and maintain connections beyond death.

Psychic hotline devotees often extend their beliefs to include broader supernatural worldviews involving destiny, karma, spirit guides, and cosmic forces that influence human events. They believe that psychics serve as intermediaries who can help them understand and work with these spiritual influences to improve their lives and achieve their goals.

Why It's Asinine

Psychic hotlines employ cold reading techniques, where operators use psychology, statistics, and conversational skills to create the impression of supernatural knowledge while gathering information from callers through leading questions and educated guesses. These techniques are well-documented psychological methods that create convincing illusions of psychic ability without requiring any supernatural powers.

Professional psychics consistently fail when tested under controlled conditions that prevent them from using cold reading techniques, gathering background information, or relying on statistical probability to make seemingly accurate statements. When genuine psychic abilities are tested scientifically, the results are consistently indistinguishable from random chance.

The business model of psychic hotlines depends on keeping callers on the phone as long as possible instead of providing accurate information or helpful guidance. Operators are trained to create dependency relationships with regular callers and to give vague advice that can be interpreted multiple ways, ensuring that customers continue calling regardless of whether predictions come true.

The supposed accuracy of psychic predictions relies on confirmation bias, where callers remember hits while forgetting misses, and on the tendency to interpret vague statements in ways that seem relevant to their personal situations. Professional psychics make broad, statistically likely statements that can apply to many people's lives, creating the illusion of personal accuracy without demonstrating supernatural knowledge.

Real research into psychic phenomena has consistently shown that claimed abilities cannot be demonstrated under controlled conditions, and that supposed psychic successes can be explained through known psychological phenomena, statistical coincidence, and the skilled application of mentalism techniques that create convincing illusions of mind reading.

My Commentary

Psychic hotlines represent the perfect intersection of exploitation and self-deception, where people pay premium rates to have strangers tell them what they want to hear while convincing themselves they're receiving supernatural guidance about their futures. These customers have turned cold reading performances into expensive therapy sessions, except their "therapists" are trained actors working from scripts designed to maximize call duration.

The psychology behind psychic hotline addiction is heartbreaking because it reveals how desperately people want certainty about uncertain futures and connection with loved ones they've lost. Instead of learning to cope with uncertainty and process grief in healthy ways, these callers become dependent on expensive fantasy conversations that promise impossible knowledge about unpredictable events.

What's cruel is how psychic hotlines exploit people during their most vulnerable moments, when they're dealing with relationship problems, financial stress, health concerns, or grief. These services market themselves as sources of hope and guidance while providing expensive entertainment that keeps customers dependent on false promises about futures that can't be predicted.

The cold reading techniques used by psychic hotline operators are impressive from a psychological standpoint, but believers mistake skilled performance for supernatural ability. These operators can create convincing illusions of mind reading using nothing more than statistical probability, careful observation of vocal cues, and conversational techniques that make callers reveal information about themselves without realizing it.

Psychic hotlines also prey on people's lack of understanding about how probability and confirmation bias work. When a psychic makes ten predictions and one turns out somewhat accurate, believers focus on the hit while forgetting the nine misses. They don't understand that making one lucky guess out of many attempts isn't evidence of supernatural ability, it's just statistics in action.

The relationship aspect of psychic hotline addiction shows how these services function more like expensive friendship simulations than genuine supernatural consultations. Regular callers often develop emotional attachments to specific psychics who remember their names and life situations, creating the illusion of personal connection while participating in a customer service performance designed to maximize revenue through repeat business.

People will pay several dollars per minute to receive advice from strangers with no credentials, training, or accountability? That shows how far people will go to avoid accepting that the future is uncertain and that some questions don't have answers. They'd pay for comforting lies instead of accepting uncomfortable truths about the unpredictability of life and the finality of death.

Chapter 12: The Power of Positive Delusion

Chapter Introduction

The universe does not care what you want. It has never read your vision board. It will not align itself with your vibrational frequency regardless of how many gratitude journals you fill. This chapter is about the multi-billion-dollar industry that disagrees.

We're diving into three spectacular examples of how people turn wishful thinking into lifestyle brands: The Secret's Law of Attraction devotees (people who think the universe responds to their thoughts like Google responds to search queries), manifestation maniacs (folks who believe they can think their way to wealth and success while ignoring basic cause and effect), and toxic positivity cultists (believers who think negative emotions are character flaws and that every tragedy contains a hidden blessing).

These beliefs aren't just psychologically damaging. They represent a fundamental misunderstanding of how reality works, plus the appealing fantasy that success requires nothing more than the right attitude and enough visualization exercises. These folks have convinced themselves that poverty is a choice, that illness results from negative thinking, and that anyone who points out problems with their philosophy is just not enlightened enough to understand cosmic law.

Behind all this lies the human desire to feel in control of uncontrollable circumstances, the seductive promise that there are simple solutions to complex problems, and the narcissistic belief that the universe revolves around individual thoughts and desires. Manifest some patience. This is going to hurt.

Manifest some patience. This is going to hurt.

The Secret's Law of Attractio Manifest some patience. This is going to hurt.

What They Believe

Law of Attraction believers claim that thoughts have magnetic properties that attract corresponding experiences, circumstances, and material objects into people's lives through universal energy fields that respond to mental vibrations. According to this philosophy, thinking about wealth attracts money, visualizing health creates physical healing, and focusing on positive relationships brings loving people into your life, while negative thoughts attract corresponding negative experiences.

These believers think the universe operates like a cosmic ordering system where thoughts function as requests that are fulfilled through mysterious but reliable mechanisms that transcend normal causation. They practice visualization exercises, create vision boards, and use affirmations to allegedly program their subconscious minds and send clear signals to the universe about what they want to manifest in their physical reality.

Law of Attraction devotees often claim that successful people throughout history have used these principles, either consciously or unconsciously, to achieve wealth, fame, and happiness. They interpret coincidences, lucky breaks, and positive outcomes as proof that their mental focus caused these events to occur, while dismissing failures as evidence that they weren't visualizing correctly or had hidden negative beliefs blocking their manifestations.

The philosophy extends to explain virtually every life circumstance through the lens of mental attraction, suggesting that people unconsciously create their own illnesses, accidents, financial problems, and relationship difficulties through improper thinking patterns. Believers often promote the idea that changing your thoughts can solve any problem and that external circumstances are merely reflections of internal mental states.

Why It's Asinine

The Law of Attraction violates basic principles of physics, psychology, and logic by proposing that thoughts can influence material reality through unexplained mechanisms that have never been scientifically demonstrated. Thoughts are electrochemical processes in the brain that have no known ability to manipulate external events, attract objects, or influence circumstances beyond their effects on the thinker's behavior and decision-making.

The supposed evidence for Law of Attraction consists entirely of anecdotal success stories, cherry-picked examples, and post hoc reasoning that ignores the role of hard work, education, opportunity, luck, and social circumstances in determining life outcomes. When subjected to controlled testing, visualization and positive thinking show no ability to influence external events beyond their psychological effects on motivation and confidence.

The philosophy's explanation for negative events is both cruel and scientifically baseless, essentially blaming victims for their circumstances by claiming they unconsciously attracted illness, poverty, or trauma through negative thinking. This victim-blaming approach ignores the complex social, economic, genetic, and environmental factors that influence health, wealth, and life circumstances.

Real success in any field requires specific skills, knowledge, effort, and often favorable circumstances that cannot be replaced by mental exercises or positive thinking. Wealthy people become wealthy through education, business skills, hard work, favorable economic conditions, and often significant advantages in family background, connections, and resources, not through visualization exercises.

The Law of Attraction industry profits by selling hope to people facing difficult circumstances while providing no reliable methods for improving their situations. Instead of encouraging productive actions like education, skill development, or strategic planning, these teachings promote passive mental exercises that waste time and energy while real problems remain unaddressed.

My Commentary

The Law of Attraction represents the ultimate triumph of magical thinking over common sense, where people have convinced themselves that the universe operates like a cosmic Amazon that delivers whatever you think about hard enough, as long as you maintain the right attitude and avoid shipping delays caused by negative thoughts. These believers have turned daydreaming into a productivity system and visualization into a career strategy.

The psychology here is wild because Law of Attraction devotees genuinely believe they can override physics, economics, and biology through sheer force of positive visualization, while dismissing every failed manifestation as user error. It's like believing that cars run on good vibes and when your car breaks down, you just weren't thinking positively enough about internal combustion engines.

What's insidious is how this philosophy turns every failure into personal responsibility and every success into cosmic validation. When believers get promotions, find love, or experience good fortune, it's proof that the universe responded to their mental vibrations. When they lose jobs, get sick, or face setbacks, it's because they had hidden negative beliefs or weren't visualizing correctly. It's a belief system that's been inoculated against reality.

The victim-blaming aspect of Law of Attraction is breathtakingly cruel because it suggests that people experiencing poverty, illness, or trauma have unconsciously attracted these circumstances through improper thinking. Cancer patients just need better thoughts, homeless people should visualize harder, and earthquake victims were broadcasting the wrong mental frequency. It's like suggesting that umbrellas cause rain because you see them during storms.

Law of Attraction turns legitimate psychological concepts like positive thinking and goal visualization into cosmic superpowers that can allegedly manipulate reality. While positive attitudes and clear goals can improve motivation and decision-making, believers have inflated these modest psychological effects into universal laws that control material circumstances through telepathic influence on quantum fields.

People will spend money on vision boards, manifestation courses, and Law of Attraction coaching instead of investing in education, skills development, or practical problem-solving? That shows how seductive the promise of effortless success can be. They'd pay for

magical thinking seminars instead of learning skills that
might improve their circumstances through boring old
cause and effect.

What They Believe

Manifestation enthusiasts claim they can bring specific desires into physical reality through focused intention, emotional alignment, and various mental techniques that supposedly communicate their wants to the universe or their subconscious minds. These practitioners believe that combining visualization, affirmations, gratitude practices, and "acting as if" they already have what they want will cause these desires to materialize through mysterious but reliable spiritual or psychological mechanisms.

Believers often practice elaborate manifestation rituals involving meditation, journaling, crystal healing, moon phases, and energy work that they think amplifies their manifesting power and helps them align with universal abundance. They create detailed lists of desired outcomes, practice emotional visualization of already having achieved their goals, and attempt to maintain high vibrational frequencies that supposedly attract positive experiences.

Modern manifestation culture incorporates elements from quantum physics terminology, neuroscience concepts, and spiritual traditions to create scientific-sounding explanations for how thoughts create reality. Practitioners claim that quantum mechanics proves that consciousness influences material reality, that neuroplasticity demonstrates the brain's ability to reshape circumstances, and that ancient wisdom traditions understood manifestation principles that modern science is rediscovering.

Manifestation believers often extend their practices to include manifesting specific people into their lives, particular job opportunities, exact amounts of money, and even changes in physical appearance or health conditions. They interpret any positive outcomes as successful manifestations while explaining failures as evidence of resistance, limiting beliefs, or misalignment with their true desires.

Why It's Asinine

Manifestation practices rely on misunderstanding and misapplication of legitimate scientific concepts like quantum mechanics and neuroplasticity, neither of which supports the claim that thoughts can directly influence external reality. Quantum effects occur at subatomic scales and have no bearing on macroscopic events, while neuroplasticity refers to the brain's ability to form new neural connections, not to reshape external circumstances through mental exercise.

The manifestation industry conflates correlation with causation by attributing positive outcomes to mental practices while ignoring the role of increased motivation, improved decision-making, and behavioral changes that often accompany goal-focused thinking. When people clarify their objectives and maintain positive attitudes, they may make better choices and notice more opportunities, but this doesn't mean their thoughts directly created external circumstances.

Real achievement in any area requires specific actions, skills, and often favorable circumstances that cannot be replaced by mental exercises or emotional alignment practices. People get jobs through qualifications and networking, build businesses through planning and execution, and improve their health through medical treatment and lifestyle changes, not through visualization and gratitude journaling.

The supposed scientific basis for manifestation claims misrepresents legitimate research findings and cherry-picks studies that seem to support predetermined conclusions while ignoring contradictory evidence. No peer-reviewed research demonstrates that meditation, visualization, or positive thinking can directly influence external events beyond their psychological effects on the practitioner.

Manifestation practices can harm people by encouraging magical thinking that replaces productive action with passive mental exercises. When people focus on manifesting outcomes instead of developing skills or taking concrete steps toward their goals, they waste time and energy on ineffective methods while real opportunities pass them by.

My Commentary

Manifestation mania represents the evolution of wishful thinking into a full-time spiritual practice, where people have convinced themselves that wanting something really, really hard while maintaining the right emotional frequency will cause the universe to rearrange itself according to their personal desires. These practitioners have turned daydreaming into a career strategy and emotional states into cosmic remote controls.

The pseudo-scientific language used by manifestation enthusiasts is hilarious because they've taken legitimate scientific concepts and turned them into magical explanations for how thoughts control reality. They throw around terms like "quantum fields" and "neuroplasticity" with the confidence of people who learned physics from inspirational Instagram posts and think that using scientific vocabulary makes their wishful thinking more credible.

What's frustrating is how manifestation culture takes the modest psychological benefits of goal-setting and positive thinking and inflates them into supernatural powers that can allegedly override economics, biology, and basic cause-and-effect relationships. While having clear goals and optimistic attitudes can improve motivation and decision-making, believers have transformed these psychological tools into cosmic ordering systems.

The ritualistic aspects of manifestation practice reveal how people can turn ordinary mental exercises into elaborate spiritual performances that make them feel productive while accomplishing nothing concrete. These folks spend hours creating vision boards, writing in gratitude journals, and aligning their chakras when they could be developing skills, networking, or taking practical steps toward their goals.

Manifestation believers often display a stunning ignorance of how the world works, imagining that they can manifest specific people into their lives, exact dollar amounts, or particular job opportunities without understanding that other people have their own agency and that economic systems operate according to principles that don't care about your emotional vibration.

Manifestation culture has spawned an entire industry of coaches, courses, and products? That shows how profitable it can be to sell people permission to believe that success requires nothing more than the right attitude and enough visualization practice. It's like a spiritual MLM scheme where the product is false hope and the compensation plan involves convincing other people to buy into magical thinking.

What They Believe

Toxic positivity advocates claim that maintaining relentlessly positive attitudes and reframing all negative experiences as opportunities for growth leads to better outcomes in life, improved mental health, and spiritual enlightenment. These believers think that negative emotions are destructive forces that should be eliminated or transformed into positive states, and that accepting difficult circumstances or expressing grief, anger, or frustration demonstrates weakness or spiritual immaturity.

Followers of toxic positivity culture promote the idea that "everything happens for a reason," that all experiences serve higher purposes, and that finding the positive aspects of traumatic events is both possible and necessary for personal development. They encourage people to "choose happiness," maintain gratitude practices during difficult times, and avoid negative thoughts or conversations that might lower their vibrational frequency or interfere with their manifestation abilities.

These believers often claim that positive thinking can prevent or cure illnesses, that optimistic people live longer and healthier lives, and that maintaining high-energy emotional states attracts better circumstances and relationships. They interpret research on the health benefits of positive emotions as proof that negativity is toxic and that people have complete control over their emotional states and life outcomes.

Toxic positivity culture extends to social media platforms where followers share inspirational quotes, gratitude posts, and success stories while avoiding discussions of problems, challenges, or systemic issues that might bring down the positive energy of their communities. They believe that focusing on solutions instead of problems and maintaining optimistic perspectives creates better outcomes for everyone involved.

Why It's Asinine

Negative emotions serve important psychological and social functions, including signaling problems that need attention, motivating necessary changes, and facilitating social bonding through shared experiences of difficulty. Attempting to eliminate or suppress these emotions can lead to psychological problems, poor decision-making, and inability to respond appropriately to real threats or challenges.

The research on positive emotions and health outcomes shows correlation, not causation, and doesn't support the claim that positive thinking can cure diseases or that negative emotions cause illness. Many factors influence health outcomes, including genetics, environmental conditions, medical care, and social circumstances that cannot be controlled through attitude adjustment or emotional regulation alone.

Toxic positivity invalidates legitimate human experiences and can be harmful to people dealing with trauma, grief, mental illness, or difficult life circumstances that require acknowledgment, processing, and appropriate response instead of positive reframing. Telling someone to "think positive" or "find the blessing" in tragedy minimizes their pain and prevents healthy emotional processing.

Real resilience and emotional health require the ability to experience and process the full range of human emotions appropriately, including negative feelings that provide important information about circumstances and relationships. People who suppress negative emotions often struggle with anxiety, depression, and relationship problems because they haven't learned to handle difficult feelings constructively.

The toxic positivity emphasis on individual attitude control ignores systemic problems, social inequalities, and environmental factors that influence life outcomes regardless of personal mindset. This individualistic focus can prevent people from seeking appropriate help, addressing real problems, or working toward necessary social changes.

My Commentary

Toxic positivity culture represents the emotional equivalent of putting a smiley face sticker on a car crash and insisting that everything is fine because you're choosing to focus on the positive aspects of vehicular disasters. These believers have turned emotional suppression into a spiritual practice and convinced themselves that feeling bad about bad things is a character flaw that prevents success and happiness.

The psychology behind toxic positivity is wild because it reveals how uncomfortable people are with the full range of human experience, preferring to live in an artificial bubble of forced optimism instead of developing the emotional skills necessary to handle life's inevitable difficulties. They've decided that negative emotions are design flaws in the human psyche that can be eliminated through sufficient attitude adjustment.

What's cruel about toxic positivity is how it invalidates legitimate suffering and turns personal tragedies into opportunities for spiritual growth seminars. These folks will tell cancer patients to be grateful for their ordeal, suggest that unemployed people should manifest better opportunities, and insist that grieving parents should find the hidden blessings in their losses. It's like emotional gaslighting disguised as motivational speaking.

The "everything happens for a reason" mythology is especially insidious because it suggests that natural disasters, violent crimes, and random accidents are all part of some cosmic plan that benefits the victims if they're spiritually mature enough to understand the lessons. This worldview requires believing that the universe deliberately inflicts suffering on people to teach them things, which is either cosmic sadism or divine incompetence.

Toxic positivity culture also creates impossible emotional standards where people feel guilty for experiencing normal human reactions to difficult circumstances. Instead of learning to process grief, anger, fear, and frustration in healthy ways, believers attempt to suppress or transform these emotions into artificial positivity that prevents genuine healing and growth.

The social media aspect of toxic positivity is nauseating because it creates performative optimism where people compete to display the most gratitude and positive energy while hiding their real struggles and authentic experiences. It's like living in a world where everyone has to pretend they're fine all the time, which is psychologically exhausting and socially isolating for anyone dealing with genuine problems.

People will pay for positivity coaching, attend happiness workshops, and buy gratitude journals instead of learning real emotional regulation skills or addressing concrete problems? That shows how seductive the promise of effortless happiness can be. They'd invest in fake positivity instead of developing the psychological tools necessary to handle real life with genuine resilience and emotional intelligence.

Chapter 13: Social Justice Buzzwords Gone Wild

Chapter Introduction

Legitimate concerns about inequality and discrimination deserve serious engagement. They also, apparently, deserve to be turned into elaborate grievance frameworks where asking someone where they're from constitutes a hate crime and wearing the wrong hairstyle is cultural theft. This chapter covers what happens when good intentions meet ideological overreach.

We're diving into four spectacular examples of how good intentions can metastasize into authoritarian thought policing: toxic masculinity hysteria (where traditional male behavior becomes pathological by definition), white privilege as original sin (turning racial awareness into a secular religion complete with confession and penance), microaggression mania (finding offense in increasingly microscopic social interactions), and cultural appropriation police (gatekeepers who determine which cultures people are allowed to appreciate based on their ancestry).

These beliefs aren't just socially divisive. They represent the transformation of legitimate social justice concerns into dogmatic systems that prioritize ideological purity over practical solutions, emotional validation over evidence-based approaches, and group identity over individual humanity. These folks have convinced themselves that progress requires constant vigilance against thought crimes, that good intentions don't matter if your identity is wrong, and that society can be perfected through sufficiently aggressive language policing.

Behind all this lies the human need to feel morally superior, the appealing simplicity of viewing complex social problems through the lens of oppressor-versus-oppressed narratives, and the addictive rush of righteous indignation that comes from identifying and punishing moral violations in others. Watch your language.

Watch your language.

Toxic Masculinity Hysteri Watch your language Watch your language.

What They Believe

Toxic masculinity theorists claim that traditional masculine traits like competitiveness, emotional restraint, physical strength, leadership, and assertiveness are inherently harmful to both men and society, representing a pathological version of manhood that must be dismantled and replaced with more emotionally expressive, collaborative, and feminized male behavior. According to these believers, masculine socialization creates men who are violent, emotionally stunted, and incapable of healthy relationships.

These advocates argue that virtually all social problems can be traced back to toxic masculine culture: domestic violence, sexual assault, workplace harassment, gun violence, war, environmental destruction, and even mental health issues stem from men being taught to suppress emotions, dominate others, and solve problems through aggression. They claim that traditional male role models perpetuate harmful stereotypes that damage both men and women.

Believers extend toxic masculinity theory to explain individual male behavior, suggesting that men who display traditional masculine traits are unconsciously perpetuating harmful gender norms even when their intentions are good. They interpret male confidence as arrogance, leadership as domination, physical strength as intimidation, and emotional control as emotional dysfunction that requires therapeutic intervention.

The movement promotes the idea that men need to be "educated" about their toxic behavior patterns and taught to embrace vulnerability, emotional expression, and collaborative approaches to life instead of competitive ones. Some versions suggest that masculinity itself is a social construct that should be eliminated in favor of more fluid gender expressions that don't reinforce patriarchal power structures.

Why It's Asinine

Traditional masculine traits like competitiveness, leadership, emotional control, and physical capability have served important social and evolutionary functions throughout human history and continue to provide value in many contexts. These characteristics aren't inherently toxic any more than traditional feminine traits are inherently beneficial. Both masculine and feminine qualities can be expressed in healthy or unhealthy ways depending on context and degree.

The theory conflates correlation with causation by attributing complex social problems to masculinity while ignoring the multiple factors that contribute to violence, aggression, and social dysfunction. Men commit more violent crimes than women, but this doesn't mean that masculine traits cause violence any more than the fact that most engineers are men means that masculinity causes mathematical ability.

Toxic masculinity theory ignores the positive contributions that traditionally masculine men make to society through leadership, protection, innovation, and hard work. Many of the institutions, technologies, and social structures that enable modern civilization were built primarily by men displaying traditional masculine characteristics like ambition, risk-taking, and competitive drive.

The approach pathologizes normal male behavior and development by treating natural masculine tendencies as disorders that require correction. Boys and men who display typical masculine traits are told they're problematic, which can damage their self-esteem and prevent them from developing healthy masculine identities that integrate both strength and emotional awareness.

Real solutions to problems like violence and relationship dysfunction require understanding the complex social, economic, psychological, and biological factors that contribute to these issues, not simply blaming masculine culture for all social ills while promoting feminized behavior as the universal solution.

My Commentary

Toxic masculinity hysteria represents what happens when legitimate concerns about male violence and emotional dysfunction get hijacked by ideologues who think the solution to bad masculine behavior is to eliminate masculine behavior entirely. These believers have decided that men are defective women who need to be reprogrammed to act more like feminists expect them to, because apparently evolution spent millions of years getting gender wrong.

The psychology here is revealing because toxic masculinity theorists seem genuinely confused about why men don't enthusiastically embrace being told that their natural tendencies are pathological and that they need to become more emotionally expressive and less competitive to be acceptable human beings. It's like telling women that femininity is toxic and they should act more like men, then wondering why they don't appreciate the helpful advice.

The attribution cuts only one way, which is where the theory falls apart: virtually every social problem gets blamed on masculine culture while the same theories ignore that traditionally masculine men built most of the civilization these critics are using to make their argument. The same competitive drive and leadership qualities that supposedly cause all social problems also built the technologies, institutions, and social structures that enable comfortable modern life, including the platforms these critics use to complain about masculinity.

The pathologizing of normal male behavior is cruel because it tells boys and men that their natural inclinations toward competition, leadership, emotional control, and physical capability are evidence of dysfunction that requires therapeutic intervention. Instead of helping men express these traits in healthy ways, toxic masculinity theory suggests they should suppress or eliminate them entirely, which is about as psychologically healthy as telling people to stop breathing.

Toxic masculinity hysteria also reveals the double standards in modern gender discussions, where feminine traits are celebrated as inherently positive while masculine traits are treated as inherently problematic. Women's emotional expression is empowerment, but men's emotional control is dysfunction. Female collaboration is wisdom, but male competition is toxicity. It's like a gender theory designed by people who think half of humanity is fundamentally broken.

Many of the people promoting toxic masculinity theory benefit from living in societies built and maintained primarily by traditionally masculine men? That shows the breathtaking ingratitude involved in this belief system. They enjoy the security, prosperity, and technological advancement created by masculine achievement while simultaneously arguing that the traits that enabled these accomplishments are harmful and should be eliminated.

What They Believe

White privilege theorists claim that white people in Western societies benefit from systemic advantages based solely on their race, and that these unearned privileges create moral obligations for white people to acknowledge their complicity in racial oppression, work to dismantle racist systems, and defer to people of color in discussions about race and social justice. According to this framework, white privilege is invisible to white people but shapes every aspect of their lives in ways they don't recognize.

Believers argue that white people must engage in ongoing self-examination and education about racism, regularly confess their privileged status, and use their advantages to amplify marginalized voices while remaining silent about their own experiences when racial topics arise. They claim that denying white privilege or expressing color-blind attitudes demonstrates unconscious racism that requires correction through anti-racism training and continued consciousness-raising.

The theory extends to suggest that white people cannot truly understand racism because their privilege prevents them from experiencing discrimination, making their perspectives on racial issues inherently limited and potentially harmful. Some versions promote the idea that white people should pay reparations, give up positions of power to people of color, and accept restrictions on their speech and behavior to compensate for historical and ongoing racial advantages.

White privilege advocates often frame opposition to their theories as evidence of white fragility, racist defensiveness, or unconscious bias that proves the very privilege they're trying to expose. They interpret any pushback against white privilege concepts as confirmation that white people are too psychologically invested in their advantages to acknowledge them honestly.

Why It's Asinine

While racial disparities exist in many areas of life, the white privilege framework oversimplifies complex social phenomena by attributing all racial differences to a single explanatory model that ignores the role of culture, individual choices, economic factors, family structure, and other variables that influence life outcomes. Many successful people of color have achieved their status through hard work and merit, not through white people giving up their privileges.

The theory creates a racial caste system where people's moral status and credibility depend on their skin color, with white people assigned permanent guilt and people of color granted moral authority based on group membership instead of individual character or knowledge. This approach contradicts principles of individual dignity and equal treatment that most people consider fundamental to justice.

White privilege theory often ignores the diversity within racial groups, treating all white people as equally privileged and all people of color as equally disadvantaged, regardless of individual circumstances like class, education, family background, or personal experiences. A poor white person from a broken family doesn't necessarily have more advantages than a middle-class black person from a stable home.

The framework can be counterproductive by creating resentment among white people who feel blamed for problems they didn't create, while encouraging learned helplessness among people of color who are told that their success depends on white people's willingness to give up advantages. This approach can undermine individual agency and interracial cooperation.

Real solutions to racial inequality require addressing specific problems through evidence-based policies and programs, not through racial consciousness-raising exercises that focus on changing attitudes instead of improving material conditions, educational opportunities, or economic circumstances that affect people's lives.

My Commentary

White privilege theory represents the transformation of racial awareness into a secular religion complete with original sin, confession rituals, and the promise of redemption through sufficient displays of guilt and self-flagellation. These believers have taken legitimate concerns about racial inequality and turned them into a moral framework where skin color determines your standing in a cosmic battle between good and evil.

The psychology behind white privilege obsession is wild because it allows people to feel morally superior while doing nothing concrete to help anyone. White privilege advocates get to experience the satisfaction of righteousness without the inconvenience of working to improve conditions for disadvantaged communities. They can confess their privilege on social media and feel like they're fighting racism without leaving their keyboards.

What's absurd is how white privilege theory treats race as both meaningless and all-important simultaneously. Race is supposedly a social construct with no biological reality, but it's also the most important factor determining every aspect of a person's life experience. Racial differences in outcomes can't be explained by cultural or individual factors, but racial identity is the only lens through which these differences can be understood.

The secular religious aspects of white privilege theory are unmistakable, from the requirement for regular confession of racial sins to the notion that salvation comes through acknowledging your inherent moral corruption and dedicating your life to serving the oppressed. It's like Christianity for people who think they're too sophisticated for religion, except the afterlife has been replaced with social media approval.

White privilege theory also creates impossible standards where white people can never do enough to prove they're not racist, while simultaneously being told that their efforts to not be racist are evidence of racism. It's a perfect Kafka trap where any response to accusations of privilege can be interpreted as confirmation of privilege, making it psychologically manipulative in ways that would make cult leaders jealous.

Many white privilege advocates are themselves privileged white people who use their racial guilt as a form of moral credentialing? That shows the narcissism involved in this belief system. They get to be the good white people who understand racism, unlike all those other white people who are too racist to acknowledge their privilege. It's virtue signaling disguised as social justice activism.

What They Believe

Microaggression theorists claim that subtle, often unconscious actions, comments, and behaviors constitute a form of discrimination that causes significant psychological harm to marginalized groups. According to this framework, seemingly innocent interactions like asking someone where they're from, complimenting someone's English, or using colorblind language constitute "death by a thousand cuts" that accumulates into serious trauma for people who experience these slights regularly.

Believers argue that microaggressions are more harmful than overt discrimination because they're harder to identify and address, leaving victims uncertain whether they experienced bias or are being oversensitive. They claim that the cumulative effect of these small slights creates hostile environments that prevent marginalized people from fully participating in education, employment, and social interactions.

The theory extends to include an ever-expanding catalog of microaggressive behaviors covering everything from tone of voice and body language to choice of words and assumptions about people's backgrounds. Advocates create detailed lists of phrases and actions that marginalized people might find offensive, along with explanations of why these behaviors perpetuate systemic oppression even when the perpetrator has no malicious intent.

Microaggression believers often promote the idea that impact matters more than intent, meaning that if someone feels harmed by an interaction, the microaggression occurred regardless of what the other person meant to communicate. They encourage marginalized people to identify and report microaggressions while educating others about how seemingly innocent behaviors can perpetuate discrimination.

Why It's Asinine

The microaggression framework pathologizes normal human interaction by treating ordinary social awkwardness, cultural differences, and innocent mistakes as forms of discrimination that cause psychological trauma. This approach encourages people to interpret ambiguous social situations through the lens of victimization instead of assuming good faith or addressing misunderstandings directly.

The theory's emphasis on subjective interpretation means that virtually any interaction can be classified as a microaggression if someone chooses to take offense, creating impossible social situations where people must constantly monitor their words and behavior for potential violations of ever-changing sensitivity standards. This hypervigilance is exhausting for everyone involved and prevents authentic relationship building.

Research on microaggressions often relies on self-reported perceptions of bias instead of objective measures of discrimination, making it difficult to distinguish between prejudice and normal social friction that gets reinterpreted through a microaggression lens. The framework also ignores how individual personality differences affect sensitivity to perceived slights.

The focus on microaggressions can distract from addressing more serious forms of discrimination and inequality by channeling energy into policing interpersonal interactions instead of working on systemic changes that would materially improve people's lives. Spending time cataloging microaggressions is less productive than addressing barriers to opportunity and advancement.

Microaggression theory can be counterproductive by increasing intergroup anxiety and tension, as people become afraid to interact naturally with members of different groups for fear of committing unintentional offenses. This can lead to more segregation and less authentic cross-cultural contact, which are necessary for reducing prejudice and building understanding.

My Commentary

Microaggression mania represents the weaponization of sensitivity, where people have taken normal human social awkwardness and transformed it into evidence of systemic oppression that requires constant vigilance and intervention. These believers have turned everyday social interactions into minefields where any misstep can be interpreted as evidence of unconscious bias that needs to be reported and corrected.

The psychology behind microaggression obsession is revealing because it shows how people can be trained to find offense in increasingly minor interactions while feeling righteous about their hypersensitivity. Instead of developing resilience and assuming good faith in ambiguous social situations, microaggression believers are encouraged to interpret every awkward interaction as evidence of discrimination.

The social standards this creates are unworkable: people are expected to navigate complex interpersonal dynamics while simultaneously running a constant internal audit for potential unconscious bias violations. Asking someone where they're from becomes a racial microaggression, complimenting someone's English becomes linguistic prejudice, and treating people equally becomes colorblind racism. It's like social interaction designed by people who hate social interaction.

The subjective nature of microaggression identification makes it the perfect tool for manufacturing grievances out of thin air. Since impact supposedly matters more than intent, anyone can claim to be victimized by virtually any interaction and demand that others modify their behavior to accommodate their personal sensitivity levels. It's emotional manipulation disguised as social justice activism.

Microaggression mania also reveals the infantilizing approach of modern social justice movements, which treat members of marginalized groups as so fragile that innocent questions about their backgrounds constitute traumatic experiences requiring institutional intervention. This approach undermines the agency and resilience of the very people it claims to protect.

Microaggression believers spend more energy cataloging and reporting minor social slights than addressing concrete barriers to opportunity? That shows how this framework can distract from meaningful social justice work. While people are having workshops about problematic language, real issues like educational inequality, economic opportunity, and criminal justice reform remain unaddressed because they require work instead of just calling out other people's insensitivity.

What They Believe

Cultural appropriation activists claim that members of dominant cultures commit a form of cultural theft when they adopt clothing, hairstyles, food, music, spiritual practices, or artistic styles from marginalized cultures without permission, understanding, or proper attribution. According to these gatekeepers, cultural borrowing becomes appropriation when it involves power imbalances, commercialization, or superficial adoption of cultural elements without respect for their original meaning or context.

Believers argue that cultural appropriation perpetuates harm by allowing privileged groups to profit from or gain social benefits from cultural elements that marginalized communities created, often while those same communities face discrimination for practicing their own traditions. They claim that seeing white people wearing dreadlocks or practicing yoga while Black people or Indians face prejudice for these same practices represents a form of cultural exploitation.

The theory extends to include detailed rules about which cultural practices different racial and ethnic groups are allowed to engage in, often based on ancestry, perceived privilege levels, and the supposed sacred or secular nature of specific cultural elements. Activists create lists of problematic appropriations while promoting "appreciation" as the acceptable alternative, though the distinction often depends on the critics' subjective judgment about the appropriator's intent and identity.

Cultural appropriation police often organize boycotts, social media campaigns, and public shaming efforts against people and businesses they believe are committing cultural theft. They frame their activities as protecting marginalized cultures from exploitation while educating privileged people about the harm their cultural borrowing causes to communities they claim to appreciate.

Why It's Asinine

Cultural exchange and borrowing have been fundamental aspects of human civilization throughout history, leading to the development of art, music, food, technology, and spiritual practices that enrich human experience across cultural boundaries. Cultures should remain separate and people can only engage with traditions based on their ancestry? That contradicts the cosmopolitan values that most people consider progressive.

The cultural appropriation framework creates artificial barriers between people based on race and ethnicity, essentially promoting cultural segregation while claiming to fight discrimination. This approach ignores how cultural practices naturally evolve and spread through human contact, often becoming enriched through cross-cultural interaction and adaptation.

The supposed harm caused by cultural appropriation is often vague and theoretical instead of concrete and measurable. While economic exploitation of indigenous artists or misrepresentation of sacred practices can cause real problems, most cultural appropriation accusations involve personal offense instead of material harm to communities or people.

Cultural appropriation policing often ignores the diversity of opinions within cultures, treating racial and ethnic groups as monolithic entities with unified positions on cultural sharing. Many members of supposedly appropriated cultures welcome and encourage cross-cultural appreciation, while others within the same communities may object to the same practices.

The framework can be counterproductive by discouraging cross-cultural understanding and appreciation, which are necessary for building diverse, inclusive societies. When people become afraid to engage with other cultures for fear of appropriation accusations, it can lead to more cultural isolation and less genuine intercultural contact.

My Commentary

Cultural appropriation policing represents the evolution of multiculturalism into cultural apartheid, where people have taken the reasonable idea that cultures deserve respect and turned it into a system of racial gatekeeping that determines which traditions people are allowed to appreciate based on their ancestry. These activists have appointed themselves as the cultural customs agents of human civilization.

The psychology behind cultural appropriation obsession reveals how people can turn appreciation into oppression by creating ever-more-complex rules about who is allowed to enjoy which aspects of human culture. Instead of celebrating how cultural exchange enriches everyone's lives, these gatekeepers focus on policing boundaries and finding offense in cross-cultural appreciation.

The intellectual property framing doesn't survive five minutes of historical scrutiny: cultural exchange and borrowing are how every human tradition has always developed, and treating culture as racially owned IP contradicts the entire history of how ideas actually travel. Jazz music, fusion cuisine, and most artistic innovations result from cultural mixing, but appropriation police want to segregate human creativity based on ancestry.

The arbitrary nature of appropriation accusations shows how this framework depends more on the critic's political opinions than any consistent principles about cultural respect. White people doing yoga is appropriation, but Japanese people wearing Western business suits is fine. Black people straightening their hair is internalized racism, but white people wearing cornrows is cultural theft. The rules change based on who's doing what to whom.

Cultural appropriation policing also ignores how most cultural practices that activists claim to protect were themselves products of earlier cultural exchange and borrowing. Traditional "Asian" martial arts incorporate techniques from multiple cultures, "authentic" Mexican food includes ingredients from Europe and Asia, and most spiritual practices combine elements from various traditions that developed through centuries of cultural contact.

Cultural appropriation activists spend more energy policing hairstyles and fashion choices than addressing concrete issues affecting marginalized communities? That shows how this framework can distract from meaningful social justice work. While people are having heated debates about who can wear what, real problems like economic inequality, educational access, and political representation remain unaddressed because they require work instead of just calling out other people's cultural choices.

Chapter 14: Red Pill Reality and Alpha Male Mythology

Chapter Introduction

At some point, legitimate frustration about masculinity in modern life collided with the internet and produced a worldview where female attraction is a stock market, society is secretly run by women, and the path to self-improvement runs through sigma male content and daily cold plunges. This chapter covers that worldview.

We're diving into four spectacular examples of how men's frustration with modern life gets channeled into pseudoscientific theories about human behavior: The Great Replacement panic (demographic anxiety disguised as civilization preservation), Sigma male grindset enthusiasts (introverts who've convinced themselves that antisocial behavior is a superior form of masculinity), women's hypergamy obsession (men who think female attraction operates like a stock market where they're penny stocks), and gynocentric society believers (folks who think men are the real oppressed gender in a world secretly controlled by women).

These beliefs aren't just socially destructive. They represent a fundamental misunderstanding of human psychology, evolutionary biology, and social dynamics, plus the appealing fantasy that there are simple explanations for complex relationship and social problems. These folks have convinced themselves that reading internet theories about alpha dominance makes them experts on human nature, that women's behavior can be decoded through evolutionary psychology memes, and that society's problems stem from men not being masculine enough.

Behind all this lies the very human need to feel important and successful, the comfort of finding external explanations for personal disappointments, and the seductive promise that adopting the right mindset and strategies can unlock the secrets to social and romantic success. The grindset begins.

The grindset begins The grindset begins.

The Great Replacement Pani The grindset begins.

What They Believe

Great Replacement theorists claim that declining birth rates among white populations in Western countries, plus increased immigration from non-European nations, represents a deliberate conspiracy to replace white majorities with non-white populations for political and economic purposes. According to these believers, liberal politicians, global elites, and various organizations are orchestrating demographic changes to create more compliant voter bases and destroy traditional Western culture.

These advocates point to statistical trends showing declining white birth rates, increasing immigration levels, and changing demographic compositions in Western cities as evidence of coordinated replacement efforts. They interpret multiculturalism policies, refugee resettlement programs, and immigration laws as deliberate tools designed to accelerate demographic transformation while suppressing white political influence and cultural dominance.

Believers often extend the theory to include claims about media manipulation, educational indoctrination, and cultural programming designed to discourage white reproduction while encouraging immigration and interracial relationships. They suggest that promoting feminism, LGBTQ rights, and career-focused lifestyles among white women serves the replacement agenda by reducing white family formation and birth rates.

The most extreme versions incorporate antisemitic elements, claiming that Jewish elites orchestrate replacement policies to weaken white nations and maintain global control. Some believers think violent resistance may be necessary to prevent demographic replacement, while others focus on encouraging white reproduction and opposing immigration through political activism.

Why It's Asinine

Demographic changes in Western countries result from complex economic, social, and cultural factors including urbanization, education levels, economic opportunities, changing social values, and individual reproductive choices, not coordinated conspiracy efforts. Birth rate declines correlate with economic development, educational advancement, and urbanization patterns that occur naturally as societies modernize.

Immigration patterns are driven primarily by economic opportunities, political instability, and family reunification instead of deliberate replacement schemes. Most immigration policies in Western countries prioritize skilled workers, family reunification, and humanitarian obligations instead of demographic manipulation for political purposes.

The theory ignores that successful immigrant integration typically involves adoption of host country values, languages, and cultural practices instead of wholesale replacement of existing cultures. Many immigrant communities become more politically and socially conservative over generations, contradicting the supposed political manipulation motives behind replacement theories.

Demographic projections showing white population decline often ignore intermarriage, changing racial classifications, and the tendency for mixed-race people to identify with multiple ethnic backgrounds. These projections also assume that current trends will continue indefinitely without considering how economic conditions, social values, and policy changes might affect future demographic patterns.

The conspiracy elements of Great Replacement theory require coordination between millions of people across different countries, political systems, and time periods while maintaining perfect secrecy about their demographic manipulation goals. This level of coordination would be impossible to achieve or maintain without credible whistleblowers or documentary evidence.

My Commentary

The Great Replacement conspiracy represents what happens when demographic anxiety meets internet echo chambers and produces elaborate theories about coordinated white genocide conducted through immigration policies and birth control advertisements. These believers have taken the normal process of social change and turned it into evidence of a cosmic plot against white civilization, because apparently multiculturalism is more threatening than nuclear weapons.

The psychology behind replacement panic is revealing because it shows how people can interpret statistical trends through paranoid lenses when they're already anxious about social change and loss of cultural dominance. Instead of accepting that societies naturally evolve through economic development, technological advancement, and cultural exchange, believers prefer to imagine shadowy conspiracies orchestrating demographic warfare.

What's absurd is how replacement theorists treat immigration and declining birth rates as if they're weapons deployed by hostile forces, while ignoring that these trends result from individual choices made by millions of people pursuing better lives, career opportunities, and personal fulfillment. Women choosing careers over large families aren't following replacement orders, they're making personal decisions about their own lives.

The antisemitic elements of replacement theory reveal how ancient prejudices get updated with modern demographic language, turning traditional scapegoating into supposedly sophisticated political analysis. These believers have repackaged centuries-old antisemitic conspiracy theories with statistical data and policy discussions, making them seem more credible to people who think citing immigration numbers makes them demographers.

Great Replacement anxiety also ignores how successful immigrant integration typically strengthens societies, contributing skills, entrepreneurship, cultural enrichment, and economic growth that benefit everyone. Demographic diversity automatically destroys civilization? That contradicts historical evidence showing how cultural mixing often produces periods of innovation and prosperity.

The violent potential of replacement theories makes them dangerous, as believers can justify extreme actions by convincing themselves they're defending civilization against coordinated destruction. When people believe their entire culture is under attack through demographic manipulation, political violence starts seeming like legitimate self-defense instead of terrorism motivated by racial hatred.

What They Believe

Sigma male advocates claim to represent a superior form of masculinity that operates outside traditional social hierarchies while achieving success through individual effort, strategic thinking, and rejection of conventional social expectations. According to this framework, sigma males are lone wolves who possess alpha-level capabilities but choose to work independently instead of competing for dominance within established social structures.

These believers promote the idea that sigma males focus on personal development, financial success, and self-improvement while avoiding the drama and competition associated with alpha-beta social dynamics. They claim that sigma males are naturally attractive to women because of their mysterious, independent nature and their refusal to seek validation or approval from others.

The sigma grindset mentality emphasizes entrepreneurship, cryptocurrency investment, fitness optimization, and various forms of self-improvement designed to achieve financial and social independence. Followers often adopt minimalist lifestyles, reject traditional relationship models, and prioritize work and personal development over social connections and conventional success markers.

Sigma male content creators promote daily routines, mindset strategies, and lifestyle choices that supposedly enable ordinary men to transcend social hierarchies and achieve extraordinary success through disciplined execution of optimized behaviors. They frame sigma identity as an elite mindset available to men who are smart and disciplined enough to reject social conditioning and pursue authentic self-actualization.

Why It's Asinine

The sigma male concept is a rebranding of introversion and social awkwardness as a superior form of masculinity that appeals to men who struggle with traditional social interactions but want to feel special about their isolation. The supposed independence and mystery of sigma males often masks social anxiety, relationship difficulties, and inability to connect authentically with others.

Real success in most areas of life requires collaboration, communication, and relationship-building skills that the sigma mindset discourages in favor of lone wolf fantasies that sound impressive but rarely produce achievements. Most successful entrepreneurs, leaders, and high achievers succeed through teamwork, networking, and social intelligence instead of mysterious independence.

The alpha-beta-sigma framework oversimplifies human personality and social behavior into convenient categories that ignore the complexity of individual differences, situational factors, and the reality that most people display different behavioral patterns in different contexts. Humans aren't wolves, and social dynamics are far more nuanced than dominance hierarchies.

The financial and lifestyle advice promoted by sigma male influencers often consists of generic self-improvement content repackaged with masculine branding to appeal to men who feel excluded from traditional success paths. Cryptocurrency investment, fitness routines, and entrepreneurship tips aren't uniquely sigma strategies, they're ordinary activities that anyone can pursue regardless of their personality type.

The sigma identity can be counterproductive by encouraging men to avoid developing the social skills, emotional intelligence, and relationship capabilities that are necessary for personal happiness and professional success. Rejecting social connection in favor of supposed independence often leads to isolation, depression, and missed opportunities for growth and fulfillment.

My Commentary

The sigma male grindset represents the evolution of social awkwardness into a lifestyle brand, where introverted men have convinced themselves that their inability to navigate social situations is evidence of superior intelligence and mysterious alpha energy that transcends ordinary human hierarchies. These guys have turned "I'm not good at parties" into "I'm too evolved for your social structures."

The psychology behind sigma identity is wild because it allows men to feel superior about their social isolation while avoiding the difficult work of developing genuine confidence and interpersonal skills. Instead of learning to connect with others authentically, sigma believers can retreat into lone wolf fantasies where their antisocial tendencies become evidence of their elite mindset.

What's hilarious is how sigma male content creators package basic self-improvement advice with mysterious masculine branding to make ordinary activities seem like secret alpha strategies. Going to the gym becomes "optimizing your physical form," avoiding social media becomes "rejecting validation seeking," and working alone becomes "transcending hierarchical competition." It's like productivity advice for people who think they're too cool for productivity advice.

The cryptocurrency and entrepreneurship obsession among sigma males reveals how these beliefs often serve as cope mechanisms for men who feel excluded from traditional success paths. Instead of developing marketable skills or building professional networks, they chase get-rich-quick schemes and imagine that their supposed sigma traits will magically translate into wealth and success.

Sigma male mythology also ignores how most genuine high achievers succeed through collaboration, mentorship, and relationship building instead of mysterious independence and rejection of social norms. The most successful entrepreneurs, artists, and leaders typically have strong social skills and extensive networks, not sigma antisocial tendencies disguised as strategic independence.

Sigma male influencers make money by selling social isolation as a superior lifestyle to socially isolated men? That shows the cruel irony of this belief system. These gurus profit from promoting independence while building their entire careers on parasocial relationships with audiences of lonely men who pay for content that reinforces their isolation.

What They Believe

Hypergamy obsessed men claim that women are biologically programmed to constantly seek relationships with higher-status males and will abandon current partners when better options become available, making all romantic relationships unstable competitions where men must continuously prove their value or risk being replaced. According to these theorists, female attraction operates like a ruthless stock market where women trade up to the highest-status males they can attract.

These believers point to evolutionary psychology concepts, divorce statistics, and dating app behavior as evidence that women's romantic choices are primarily driven by status, resources, and genetic quality instead of emotional connection or compatibility. They argue that women's stated preferences for kindness, humor, and emotional connection are either self-deception or deliberate misdirection designed to extract resources from lower-value males.

The hypergamy framework extends to explain various relationship phenomena: why women initiate most divorces, why female attraction can seem inconsistent, why some women date multiple men simultaneously, and why relationships fail when men lose jobs, become ill, or experience other status reductions. Believers claim that understanding hypergamy allows men to develop strategies for attracting and retaining female partners.

Many advocates promote the idea that men should focus on increasing their "sexual market value" through wealth accumulation, physical fitness, social status, and game strategies designed to trigger women's hypergamous instincts. Some versions suggest that long-term monogamous relationships are impossible because women's hypergamous nature will eventually lead them to seek superior partners.

Why It's Asinine

While mate selection preferences exist in humans as in other species, reducing female romantic behavior to simple hypergamous calculations ignores the complexity of human attraction, which involves emotional compatibility, shared values, physical chemistry, timing, and numerous other factors that vary significantly between people and relationships.

The evolutionary psychology theories cited by hypergamy believers often misrepresent legitimate research by cherry-picking studies that seem to support predetermined conclusions while ignoring contradictory evidence and the complexity of human behavioral evolution. Most evolutionary psychologists emphasize that human behavior results from multiple evolutionary pressures and significant individual variation.

Real relationship data shows that most successful long-term partnerships involve compatibility across multiple dimensions including emotional, intellectual, physical, and practical factors instead of simple status calculations. Many women choose partners based on emotional connection, shared goals, and compatibility instead of maximizing male status or resources.

The hypergamy obsession ignores how men also make strategic romantic choices based on attractiveness, fertility signals, and other evolutionary factors, while simultaneously judging women for supposedly making strategic choices. The framework applies different moral standards to male and female romantic behavior while claiming to describe universal biological patterns.

Research on relationship satisfaction and stability shows that factors like communication skills, emotional intelligence, shared values, and mutual respect predict relationship success better than male status or female hypergamous behavior. Focusing exclusively on status competition instead of developing relationship skills typically leads to poor romantic outcomes.

My Commentary

Women's hypergamy obsession represents what happens when men who struggle with dating discover evolutionary psychology memes and convince themselves that female attraction is a conspiracy against average guys orchestrated by millions of years of natural selection. These believers have turned their romantic disappointments into a scientific theory about female nature that conveniently explains why women don't appreciate their obvious superiority.

The psychology behind hypergamy fixation is revealing because it allows men to avoid taking responsibility for their romantic failures by blaming women's supposedly ruthless biological programming instead of examining their own social skills, emotional intelligence, or relationship capabilities. It's easier to theorize about female nature than to develop the personal qualities that make someone genuinely attractive.

What's absurd is how hypergamy believers treat women like stock market algorithms while simultaneously complaining that women don't appreciate their authentic selves. They want to be loved for who they are while viewing female romantic choices as calculated status optimization, apparently unaware that constantly analyzing women's behavior through the lens of biological determinism might not be the most attractive personality trait.

The evolutionary psychology misinterpretation is hilarious because these guys have taken complex research about human behavioral tendencies and reduced it to simple rules about female gold-digging and male competition. They've turned dating into a video game where knowing the female programming codes gives them cheat access to romantic success.

Hypergamy obsession also reveals how these beliefs function as elaborate cope mechanisms for men who feel inadequate in modern dating environments. Instead of developing confidence, social skills, or emotional maturity, they can blame their lack of romantic success on women's impossible biological standards and society's failure to recognize their true value.

Men who constantly worry about women's hypergamous instincts often display the exact personality traits that make them unattractive: insecurity, resentment, transactional thinking about relationships, and inability to connect authentically with women as individual human beings instead of biological programs executing evolutionary strategies.

What They Believe

Gynocentric society theorists claim that modern Western societies have become systematically biased in favor of women's interests and perspectives while discriminating against men through legal systems, educational institutions, workplace policies, and cultural narratives that prioritize female experiences and outcomes. According to these believers, feminism has created a social structure where men face systemic disadvantages while women enjoy unearned privileges.

These advocates point to statistics showing male disadvantages in education completion, criminal justice outcomes, mental health support, domestic violence recognition, and family court decisions as evidence that society has overcorrected for historical gender inequality and now systematically favors women. They argue that men's issues are ignored or minimized while women's concerns receive disproportionate attention and resources.

The theory extends to claim that cultural narratives consistently portray men as perpetrators and women as victims, creating social expectations that men should sacrifice their own interests for women's benefit while receiving little appreciation or reciprocal support. Believers suggest that male disposability is built into social systems that value female safety and well-being above male lives and welfare.

Gynocentric theorists often promote the idea that feminism has evolved beyond equality into female supremacy, using institutional power to advance women's interests at men's expense while maintaining victim narratives that prevent recognition of men's legitimate grievances and social contributions. Some versions suggest that reversing gynocentric bias requires organized male advocacy and conscious rejection of feminist frameworks.

Why It's Asinine

While men face legitimate issues in areas like education, mental health, and family court outcomes, attributing these problems to systematic pro-female bias oversimplifies complex social phenomena that result from multiple factors including traditional gender roles, economic changes, and institutional practices that affect both genders in different ways.

The gynocentric framework ignores that women continue to face significant disadvantages in many areas including political representation, corporate leadership, wage gaps in many fields, and safety concerns that affect their daily lives and career choices. Social progress for women doesn't automatically create systematic bias against men.

Many of the male disadvantages cited by gynocentric theorists result from traditional masculine expectations and social roles instead of feminist policies. Higher male suicide rates, educational disengagement, and criminal justice disparities often relate to masculine cultural norms that discourage help-seeking behavior and emotional expression instead of systematic female privilege.

The theory conflates increased attention to women's issues with systematic discrimination against men, ignoring that addressing historical inequalities often requires targeted efforts that may temporarily seem to favor previously disadvantaged groups. Affirmative action and women-focused programs aren't evidence of gynocentrism, they're attempts to level playing fields that were previously tilted.

Real solutions to men's issues require understanding the specific factors that contribute to problems like educational disengagement, mental health challenges, and social isolation instead of simply blaming feminist influence for all male disadvantages while demanding that society prioritize men's concerns over women's needs.

My Commentary

Gynocentric society claims represent what happens when legitimate concerns about male mental health and social problems get hijacked by men who think the solution to their issues is convincing everyone that women have it too good and men are the real victims of modern gender politics. These believers have created a victim hierarchy where male problems can only be addressed by proving that women aren't really oppressed.

The psychology behind gynocentric obsession is wild because it allows men to feel victimized by women's social progress while avoiding the difficult work of addressing the factors that contribute to male disadvantages. It's easier to blame feminism for male suicide rates than to examine how traditional masculine expectations prevent men from seeking mental health support.

What's absurd is how gynocentric theorists interpret any attention to women's issues as evidence of systematic bias against men, as if society has a finite amount of concern that gets depleted when women receive support. They view gender equality as a zero-sum competition where women's gains automatically become men's losses, apparently unaware that many gender issues affect both sexes.

The victim competition aspect is revealing because gynocentric believers seem more interested in proving that men have it worse than women than in developing effective solutions to male problems. They spend more energy arguing about who faces more discrimination than working to address educational disengagement, mental health stigma, or social isolation that affect men's lives.

Gynocentric claims also ignore how many feminists support addressing men's issues when they're discussed as genuine social problems instead of weapons in gender wars. Men's mental health, educational engagement, and emotional development are legitimate concerns that deserve attention, but framing them as evidence of female privilege prevents productive collaboration.

Men who constantly complain about gynocentric bias often display the exact attitudes that make it difficult to build support for men's issues: resentment toward women, zero-sum thinking about gender equality, and inability to discuss male problems without blaming feminism for creating them. This approach alienates potential allies while reinforcing stereotypes about male victimhood mentality.

Chapter 15: Logical Fallacies That Fuel Ridiculous Beliefs

Chapter Introduction

Everything in this book has one thing in common. Not the specific beliefs — those range from "the Earth is flat" to "bleach is medicine" to "birds are government drones." Not the people holding them, who span every demographic and education level. What they share is the reasoning machinery underneath. Every spectacular failure of logic we've encountered in the previous fourteen chapters runs on the same small set of broken engines, recycled endlessly, applied to whatever the believer happens to be convinced of this week.

These aren't exotic failures. They're the predictable, catalogued, well-documented ways human brains take shortcuts when they should be doing actual work. Logicians named them in Latin two thousand years ago. They still work perfectly today, which tells you something depressing about how much we've learned.

This chapter is the autopsy report. Here are the specific reasoning errors that power every ridiculous belief in this book, explained through the actual people making them, so you can recognize the engine even when the vehicle looks different.

The False Dichotomy

The false dichotomy is the Swiss Army knife of the intellectually dishonest. It takes any situation with fifty possible answers and presents you with exactly two — both extreme, both theatrical, and both designed to make you forget the other forty-eight exist.

The vaccine conspiracists have perfected this. Your choices are: Big Pharma wants to microchip your children and owns your doctor, or you're a brainwashed sheep who'll inject anything a white coat hands you. There is no third option. There is no "vaccines are medically beneficial with a small, well-documented risk profile that we monitor through rigorous surveillance systems." That answer is too boring to generate engagement and too nuanced to fit on a protest sign.

The flat earthers do the same thing in reverse. Either NASA and every government on Earth has been running the most elaborate geographic deception in human history for no clear reason, or you're asleep and too conditioned by the education system to see the truth. These are the only two positions available. The possibility that you could examine satellite imagery, understand orbital mechanics, and simply conclude the Earth is spherical because the evidence for that conclusion is overwhelming? Not on the menu.

Climate change deniers work this angle beautifully: either climate change is a socialist hoax designed to destroy capitalism and hand power to a global elite, or we must immediately abolish all fossil fuels, return to subsistence farming, and sacrifice the economy on the altar of radical environmentalism. The actual middle ground — that climate change is real, serious, and addressable through a range of technological, economic, and policy approaches that don't require anyone to stop eating or flying — gets crowded out by the two dramatic extremes.

What makes this fallacy so durable is that it feels decisive. Choosing between two options feels like being a person with convictions. Saying "it depends, and here are the relevant factors" feels like waffling, which feels like weakness, which feels like being one of them. So people take the clean answer, the dramatic answer, the answer that puts them clearly on a side — and reality, which stubbornly refuses to organize itself into two teams, gets ignored entirely.

The conspiracy theorist version is my personal favorite because it's the cleanest expression of the form. Either the official story is true and you're asleep, or the truth is what they've figured out and you're awake. There is no third position available. There is no "the official explanation is mostly accurate with some details we're still working through." There is no "complex events sometimes have complex, overlapping causes." Complexity is for cowards. Binary is for people who've done the research.

Cherry-Picking Evidence

Cherry-picking is what happens when someone has already decided what they believe and needs to find the evidence to match. The conclusion arrives first. The supporting data gets assembled afterward, selectively, like decorating a room after choosing the furniture — everything that fits goes in, everything that clashes gets left in the hallway.

The flat earthers are Olympic-level practitioners. They'll cite the Bedford Level experiment from 1838 — where a man stood by a canal, squinted at some boats, and declared Earth must be flat because he couldn't see curvature — while simultaneously dismissing satellite imagery, GPS technology, time zones, stellar parallax, and the entire body of physics built on the assumption that Earth is a sphere. All of that evidence is fabricated or misunderstood. The canal squinting was real. The selection process here is not subtle.

Homeopathy believers do the same thing with medical research. The field of homeopathy has been studied extensively. The overwhelming conclusion from dozens of systematic reviews involving hundreds of trials is that it performs no better than placebo. Believers are aware of this body of research. They have decided it's wrong. What they cite instead are isolated studies with small sample sizes, methodological problems, and results that haven't been replicated — which is to say, exactly the kind of evidence that scientists discount as noise. To a cherry-picker, it's gold.

The QAnon crowd turned this into an art form with their Q drops. Any world event that could plausibly be read as confirmation of the theory got added to the evidence pile. Events that contradicted the theory got explained away — the deep state intervened, the timeline shifted, disinformation was necessary. This is not a belief system that interacts with evidence. It's a belief system that absorbs evidence and converts it all into confirmation. Feed it data that supports the theory and it grows. Feed it data that contradicts the theory and it also grows, because contradiction just means the conspiracy is bigger than you thought.

The thing about cherry-picking that makes it so hard to argue with is that the cherries are real. The Bedford Level experiment happened. There are isolated vaccine studies with concerning findings. There are Q drops that made vague predictions about political events. The believer isn't making things up — they're selecting, and selection is invisible from the inside. They genuinely believe they've done the research. They have. They've done thorough, comprehensive research into the evidence that supports their conclusion, and they've dismissed everything else as contaminated. This is what they call critical thinking.

The Appeal to Nature

"Natural" is the most successful marketing word in the English language and the most useless word in the English language, because it means nothing. Arsenic is natural. Smallpox is natural. The Bubonic plague swept across Europe naturally and killed a third of the population in a completely organic and chemical-free process. Nature does not care about you. Nature is trying to eat you.

This has not stopped an entire alternative medicine industry from building itself entirely on the premise that natural equals good and synthetic equals suspicious. Homeopathy: natural. Crystal healing: literally rocks, could not be more natural. Urine therapy: about as natural as it gets, your own body produced it. None of these work. Meanwhile, chemotherapy — synthetic, developed in a laboratory, involves chemicals with long names nobody can pronounce — extends the lives of cancer patients by years and sometimes decades. The believer rejects it.

Urine therapy is where this fallacy reaches its purest expression. Your body produced it, therefore it's good to drink back. By this logic, everything your body excretes is a potential health supplement. Your kidneys filtered it out specifically because your body was done with it. The body has opinions about what belongs inside it and what needs to leave. Urine therapy requires believing the kidneys are wrong.

The anti-vaccine movement runs this play constantly. Natural immunity is real immunity, acquired the honest way, through the immune system doing its job. Vaccine-induced immunity is artificial, a shortcut, a chemical intrusion into your body's natural processes. Never mind that "natural" immunity to smallpox required surviving smallpox, and surviving smallpox was not something everyone managed. Never mind that the body's natural response to measles includes a one-in-a-thousand chance of encephalitis. Natural, in this framing, is automatically preferable to effective.

What makes the appeal to nature especially funny is that it's only applied selectively. Nobody in the crystal healing community is refusing to drive cars, use electricity, or drink treated water. Nobody promoting natural immunity is refusing antibiotics when they get a serious infection. The "natural is better" principle gets applied to vaccines and medicine and food, where it causes genuine harm, and quietly suspended everywhere else, where it would cause inconvenience.

Post Hoc Ergo Propter Hoc

Latin for "after this, therefore because of this." Which is a sophisticated way of saying: a thing happened, then another thing happened, therefore the first thing caused the second thing. Babies are born nine months after Valentine's Day. Valentine's Day causes babies. You started taking your crystal supplements and your headache went away. The crystals cured your headache. You watched a flat earth documentary and two weeks later read something confusing about GPS. The documentary proved something.

This is the engine under most of alternative medicine. You felt terrible, you tried the remedy, you felt better. The remedy worked. The alternative explanations — you were at the peak of the illness and would have recovered anyway, you also rested and drank water, the placebo effect is real and powerful, most conditions resolve on their own — don't register, because the sequence was: remedy, then better. What other explanation could there be?

Parents in the anti-vaccine movement built an entire global movement on post hoc reasoning. Their child received a vaccine. Shortly afterward, their child showed signs of autism. The vaccine caused the autism. This reasoning was so compelling, so emotionally undeniable, that it overwhelmed twenty years of epidemiological research involving millions of children, the retraction of the original fraudulent study, and the loss of the original researcher's medical license. The sequence felt like proof. The sequence was not proof. The sequence was coincidence, which looks identical to causation from the inside.

Psychic hotlines have made billions of dollars off this fallacy. You called the psychic. You felt better. The psychic helped you. The psychic also said twelve things that were wrong and you don't remember those. You remember the things that seemed accurate. The session ended, life continued, some things went well. The psychic predicted good things would come. Good things came. The psychic was right.

The post hoc fallacy is particularly vicious because it's not irrational in most everyday contexts. If you eat a strange mushroom and then become violently ill, assuming the mushroom caused your illness is a reasonable and potentially survival-relevant inference. The problem comes when people apply that same logic to situations with complex causal chains, time delays, and multiple confounding factors — which is to say, basically every interesting question in medicine, health, economics, and human behavior. The brain that saved your ancestor from poisonous mushrooms is now crediting magic water for curing your cold.

Ad Hominem

The ad hominem attack is what people use when they don't have an argument. Instead of addressing the evidence or the logic, you address the person presenting it. You attack their motives, their funding sources, their character, their affiliations. If the person can be discredited, the argument disappears. You never have to engage with the actual substance.

The conspiracy community has built an entire epistemological system around this fallacy. When a scientist publishes research showing vaccines are safe, they're a paid shill for pharmaceutical companies. When a doctor recommends chemotherapy, they're financially incentivized to keep patients sick. When a climate researcher presents evidence of warming, they're chasing grant money in a corrupt system that only funds predetermined conclusions. The argument becomes: every credentialed expert in the relevant field has corrupt motives, therefore their expertise is worthless, therefore the YouTube video made by a guy in his garage is equally valid.

This is elegant because it makes the credential itself suspicious. The more expertise you have in a field, the more you've been captured by the corrupt system that field is embedded in. The less expertise you have, the more you can be trusted, because you're an outsider with nothing to gain. This is a framework that specifically rewards ignorance, which may explain why it's popular in communities that celebrate doing their own research rather than listening to people who've spent their careers on the question.

The flat earthers are particularly committed to this. NASA's satellite imagery proves Earth is spherical. NASA is a government agency that lies. Therefore the imagery is fabricated. Every pilot, navigator, and astronaut who could testify to Earth's shape has either been deceived themselves or is in on the conspiracy. Every physicist who explains why a flat earth model can't account for gravity, time zones, or the behavior of GPS satellites is either ignorant or compromised. The evidence doesn't matter. Only the source matters. And every source with relevant knowledge has a reason to lie.

What's telling about the ad hominem in these contexts is how selectively it gets applied. The same person who dismisses peer-reviewed research because it's funded by pharmaceutical companies will uncritically share a Facebook post from someone selling supplements. The corruption of expertise only flows one direction. The experts who support your conclusion are brave truth-tellers. The experts who contradict it are paid shills. The methodology for determining which category someone falls into is simply whether they agree with you.

Confirmation Bias and the Art of Never Being Wrong

Confirmation bias is the grandfather of all the fallacies above, because it's the reason people keep using them. You've already decided what you believe. Your brain helpfully highlights evidence that supports it and downplays evidence that doesn't. You're not lying to yourself — you're not even aware it's happening. The filtering is automatic, invisible, and feels like common sense.

The QAnon movement built an entire prophecy system that has never made a correct specific prediction and has never been wrong once in its followers' minds. Predicted dates pass without the promised events. The explanation: disinformation was necessary to confuse the enemy. The timeline shifted. It happened, just not publicly yet. Every failed prediction becomes evidence of a more complex and sophisticated operation than originally understood. The theory absorbs contradictions and grows stronger. This is confirmation bias weaponized into a belief system that has literally been vaccinated against reality.

The manifestation community runs the same logic with slightly better aesthetics. You visualized your goals and good things happened: manifestation works. You visualized your goals and nothing happened: you had hidden negative beliefs, your frequency was misaligned, you didn't really believe it, you were manifesting from a place of lack rather than abundance. There is no outcome that constitutes a failed test. There is only manifestation that worked and manifestation that hasn't happened yet.

What confirmation bias really reveals is how expensive it is to change your mind. Not financially — psychologically. If you've built your identity around a belief, if you've organized your social circle around it, if you've based major decisions on it, then admitting you were wrong doesn't just update an idea. It threatens who you are. The belief and the self become the same thing. Attacking one attacks the other. So the brain protects both.

This is why presenting flat earthers with satellite imagery makes them more confident in the flat earth theory. The satellite imagery is evidence the conspiracy is real and powerful enough to fake convincing photos. This is why presenting anti-vaccine parents with safety data strengthens their opposition. The safety data is evidence of how thoroughly the pharmaceutical industry has corrupted the research establishment. Every piece of contradictory evidence becomes confirmation. It's the most perfect closed system ever devised, and it runs in every human brain, including yours and mine, any time we care enough about the conclusion to protect it.

The Logical Fallacy Ecosystem

These fallacies don't operate in isolation. They form a system. The false dichotomy creates the dramatic choice. Cherry-picking provides the supporting evidence. The appeal to nature offers the simple decision rule. Post hoc reasoning creates the personal experience of success. Ad hominem disposes of the inconvenient experts. And confirmation bias filters everything through the preferred conclusion, ensuring nothing that enters the system can disturb it.

By the time you've got all six running simultaneously, you've built something that is genuinely impervious to rational argument from the outside. The flat earth community isn't a collection of stupid people making obvious mistakes. They're normal people running normal cognitive machinery in a closed loop that has been optimized over years of practice to produce a single output: the Earth is flat. The machinery works fine. The inputs are controlled. The output is predetermined.

Understanding these fallacies won't make you immune to them. I use them. You use them. Everyone does, about something, because they're features of how human cognition works under pressure, not bugs you can patch out. What you can do is slow down when you notice you're reaching for them — particularly when you're reaching for the one that lets you dismiss an expert without engaging with their argument, or the one that lets you reframe a failed prediction as confirmation of success, or the one that tells you the only two options are the two that make your side look heroic.

That pause is the entire difference between critical thinking and its convincing imitation.

Chapter 16: The Echo Effect of Social Media and Fast Communication

Chapter Introduction

Imagine you could build a machine specifically designed to make people believe ridiculous things. You'd want it to show people content that confirms what they already think, hide content that might make them reconsider, reward the most extreme and emotionally provocative claims with maximum visibility, and make it almost impossible to distinguish between a credentialed expert and a person who watched some videos last night. You'd want it to connect every person who believes something weird with every other person who believes the same thing, so they can all reinforce each other simultaneously, across every time zone, at the speed of light.

You'd want to make sharing feel good — like a hit of something, a small chemical reward that encourages you to keep going, keep posting, keep spreading the thing you just found, before you've had time to check whether it's real.

You'd want corrections and rebuttals to perform worse than the original false claim, so that when someone points out that the thing was wrong, almost nobody sees it.

Congratulations. You just invented Facebook. You also invented YouTube, Twitter, Instagram, TikTok, and most of the rest of the modern internet. Nobody sat down and designed these platforms as misinformation engines — they were designed to maximize engagement. The misinformation problem is just what engagement optimization looks like when you point it at human psychology.

This chapter is about how that machine operates, and how it turned every ridiculous belief in this book from a fringe curiosity held by a handful of people into an organized movement with its own internal logic, vocabulary, community structures, and resistance to outside correction.

The Algorithm Does Not Know What Is True

The algorithm knows what gets clicked. These are not the same thing.

Social media platforms run on engagement — the total volume of clicks, comments, shares, and time spent that a piece of content generates. Engagement is how they make money, because engagement means eyeballs, and eyeballs means advertising revenue. The algorithm's entire purpose is to maximize engagement, which means it shows people content that generates engagement, which means it shows people content that makes them click, comment, share, and keep scrolling.

Turns out the things that make people click, comment, share, and keep scrolling are not primarily accurate things. They're emotionally arousing things. Outrage is arousing. Fear is arousing. Tribal validation — the feeling that you've found your people, that your side is right, that the other side is evil or stupid — is deeply arousing. Nuanced analysis of complex policy tradeoffs is not arousing. A calm explanation of why the vaccine schedule is safe doesn't get shares. A video claiming vaccines cause autism and doctors are hiding it gets shares, comments, angry reactions, and furious rebuttals, all of which count as engagement, all of which signal to the algorithm that this content is performing well and should be shown to more people.

This is why a flat earth conference gets more YouTube views than an astronomy lecture. The flat earth conference is emotionally compelling. It has drama, it has a villain (NASA), it has a persecuted truth-teller narrative, and it flatters the viewer's sense of themselves as someone smart enough to see through the official story. The astronomy lecture explains how stars work. The algorithm cannot tell the difference between these in terms of truthfulness. It can tell the difference in terms of engagement. The flat earth conference wins.

Nobody at YouTube or Facebook decided this was fine. They built systems that optimized for a metric that happened to correlate with the spread of misinformation. The effect was the same as if they'd decided it on purpose.

The Rabbit Hole Is a Feature

If you watch one flat earth video on YouTube, the algorithm immediately recommends ten more flat earth videos. Not because YouTube loves flat earthers, but because you just demonstrated a revealed preference: you are a person who watches flat earth content. The algorithm's job is to keep you watching, and the fastest path to keeping you watching is more of what you just watched. Within a few sessions, your recommended feed is saturated with flat earth content, and the evidence that Earth is spherical has essentially vanished from your information environment.

This is how people who "just got curious" about vaccine safety end up, six months later, convinced that pharmaceutical companies are murdering children for profit. Each piece of content leads to the next. The next is always slightly more extreme, because content that went slightly further generated slightly more engagement, so the algorithm slightly prefers it. The journey doesn't require a conspiracy or a recruiter. It just requires watching videos at night and letting the next one autoplay.

QAnon grew this way. People who were vaguely suspicious of political elites found content that confirmed their suspicion. The algorithm recommended more. The more they watched, the more extreme the content the algorithm served. By the time people had been in the rabbit hole for six months, they'd arrived at adrenochrome harvesting and secret military tribunals that had been conducted without anyone's knowledge, and this didn't seem crazy because they'd been walked to it gradually, one autoplay at a time, in a closed environment where everyone they encountered agreed.

The anti-vaccine movement found its mass audience through Facebook groups. Isolated parents who'd had concerns found each other. The group provided community, emotional validation, shared stories of damaged children, and a collective framework for interpreting every piece of contrary evidence as Big Pharma propaganda. The group also had no mechanism for correction — no editor, no peer review, no outside voice. It was a closed system designed to reinforce its own conclusions. Membership grew, the shared beliefs intensified, and the algorithm kept sending more people in because the group had strong engagement numbers.

"I've done my research" means something specific in the internet age. It means: I have found content that supports the conclusion I already had, and I have consumed a lot of it. This is not what research means. Research involves seeking disconfirming evidence, evaluating methodology, checking sources, and being willing to follow the evidence to a conclusion you didn't expect and might not like. "I've done my research" means the opposite of this. It means the investigation was conducted with the conclusion already in hand, and the purpose was to furnish that conclusion with ammunition.

The internet makes this trivially easy. If you believe that 5G towers cause cancer, there are hundreds of websites that will provide you with articles, citations, expert opinions, and scientific-sounding arguments supporting that conclusion. They are not peer-reviewed. They have not been replicated. The citations, if you trace them, lead to other websites citing the same discredited studies. But they look exactly like research. They're formatted like research. They have footnotes.

The same person who dismisses the entire peer-reviewed literature on vaccine safety because it's "funded by pharmaceutical companies" will share a paper from a journal they've never heard of, written by a researcher affiliated with an institution that doesn't appear to exist, published six months ago, and treat it as definitive evidence. The credibility filter runs backwards. Establishment sources are corrupt. Alternative sources are brave. The methodology for determining which category a source falls into is simply whether it confirms the belief.

This is how the chemtrail conspiracy acquired its vocabulary of atmospheric chemistry. This is how the

MMS advocates developed their protocols for chlorine dioxide dosing. This is how flat earthers constructed their competing models of disc physics and polar geometry. The internet provided the raw material. "Doing research" assembled it into something that looked like a knowledge base, and the algorithm ensured it never encountered a serious challenge.

The Influencer as Medical Authority

Dr. Oz sold more medical misinformation to more people than almost any other single source in American history, and he spent decades doing it on television before anyone could reliably call it out. He was a heart surgeon. He had credentials. He spoke confidently about things outside his expertise — supplements, alternative therapies, miracle cures — to an audience of tens of millions of people who trusted him because he was a doctor, he was on TV, and he seemed to know what he was talking about.

The internet has produced thousands of influencers with none of the credential requirements and none of the broadcast network oversight. Any person who is photogenic, confident, emotionally relatable, and willing to tell audiences what they want to hear can build a following of millions. They don't need to be right. They need to be engaging. The algorithm handles the rest.

The wellness influencer who promotes juice cleanses, crystal healing, and vaccine skepticism to her two million Instagram followers is not a doctor. She is someone who learned to talk about health in a way that resonates with the anxieties of her audience: the sense that modern medicine is impersonal and profit-driven, that nature is healing, that you can take control of your own health if you just know the right things. Her audience trusts her not because she's right but because she feels real. She shares her children's photos. She documents her own health journey. She responds to comments. She is present in a way that a distant oncologist isn't.

What makes this dangerous isn't that influencers are malicious. Most of them are not. They believe what they're saying. They built their platforms on authenticity, which means their conviction is genuine — and genuine conviction is the most persuasive thing in the world, regardless of whether the conviction is warranted.

When someone with two million followers says she stopped vaccinating her children after doing extensive research, those two million people receive the information embedded in a relationship they've built with this person over months or years. It doesn't feel like propaganda. It feels like trusted advice from someone who knows them, cares about their children, and has done the work so they don't have to.

Misinformation at the Speed of Light

A lie travels around the world before the truth has got its boots on. This was true in Samuel Johnson's time. In 2026 it's not a metaphor; it's a testable measurement. Studies of Twitter found that false information spreads six times faster than true information. False information is more novel, more emotionally engaging, and more shareable than true information. True information is often boring. It says: the situation is complicated, the evidence is mixed, conclusions should be held with appropriate uncertainty. That doesn't spread. It doesn't generate clicks. It doesn't get retweeted.

The Sandy Hook shooting was followed within hours by conspiracy theories claiming the children were crisis actors, the parents were performing grief, and the whole thing was a false flag operation to promote gun control. These theories reached millions of people on the day of the shooting, in the hours when the facts were still unclear and the emotional shock was at its peak. The corrections — that the children were real, the shooting was real, the grief was real, the "actors" were parents who had just buried their seven-year-olds — came days and weeks later, spread to a fraction of the audience, and performed a fraction of the engagement. By then the false narrative had been watched, shared, and integrated into the belief systems of millions of people who would never see the correction.

COVID-19 misinformation spread faster than the virus. By the time health authorities had confirmed basic facts about transmission and severity, the internet had already deployed several competing narratives: the virus was a bioweapon, the virus was a hoax, the lockdowns were a cover for 5G rollout, hydroxychloroquine cured it, bleach could prevent it, Bill Gates had engineered it as a pretext to inject tracking chips into the global population. Some of these narratives will never be fully corrected in the minds of the people who absorbed them first. The first story wins, because the first story gets read when the audience is maximally uncertain and maximally frightened, and frightened people absorb information differently.

The Correction Nobody Sees

The most insidious feature of the misinformation ecosystem is what happens after something gets debunked. The debunking rarely reaches the same people who saw the original claim. It generates less engagement

— it's not as emotionally satisfying to learn that a thing was wrong as it is to learn that a dramatic thing happened. The algorithm doesn't prioritize it. It goes into a database somewhere, referenced by journalists and fact-checkers, essentially invisible to the community that absorbed the original false claim.

The QAnon followers who believed that on a specific date in 2021 Donald Trump would be reinstated as president did not, when that date passed uneventfully, update their belief systems and move on. They adjusted the timeline, proposed that an underground operation was still in progress, and continued. The specific prediction was wrong. The theory absorbed the failure and grew larger. The mechanism for correction — demonstrating that a prediction was wrong — doesn't work on a system that has preemptively inoculated itself against correction by categorizing every failure as part of a more sophisticated operation.

This is the closed loop at the heart of the social media misinformation problem. The platforms amplify the claim. The claim reaches millions. The correction reaches thousands. The people who believe the claim are embedded in communities that provide social, emotional, and epistemic support for continued belief. The correction feels like an attack from the enemy. The correction makes them believe harder.

You can't fix this from the outside. The people inside the loop don't experience themselves as being in a loop. They experience themselves as having finally found the truth, after years of being deceived by mainstream sources, surrounded by people who've done the same work and arrived at the same conclusions. That's not a description of a cult. That's a description of what it feels like to be in a cult.

The Perfect Storm

Social media didn't create flat earthers, anti-vaxxers, or manifestation gurus. These beliefs existed before the internet. What the internet did was find every person who held one of these beliefs in isolation and connect them to every other person who held the same belief, remove the social friction that previously made it embarrassing to say publicly that you think the moon landing was faked, give them the tools to create and share content that looks authoritative, and then show that content to everyone who had ever expressed similar interests, algorithmically sorted by what would generate the most engagement.

The result is not just that more people believe ridiculous things. It's that the people who believe ridiculous things are now organized, productive, and mutually reinforcing in ways they couldn't have been twenty years ago. A flat earther in 1995 was alone, probably embarrassed, possibly aware at some level that their belief was socially untenable. A flat earther in 2026 has a community, a movement, annual conferences, merchandise, YouTube celebrities, and the shared emotional certainty that comes from having ten thousand people confirm your most important beliefs every time you open your phone.

We built a machine that was very good at making that happen. We should probably think carefully about that.

Chapter 17: Cognitive Biases Behind the Madness

Chapter Introduction

Here is the genuinely unsettling thing: the people in this book are not stupid. I know that's not what you were expecting me to say after three hundred pages of detailed evidence that they are doing very stupid things. But the flat earthers include engineers. The anti-vaccine movement has recruited pediatricians. The QAnon community has absorbed lawyers, teachers, military officers, and people with graduate degrees. The bleach advocates are sometimes former medical professionals. The manifestation industry was built substantially by people intelligent enough to make it a multi-billion-dollar business.

The problem is not intelligence. The problem is that intelligence is a tool, and like any tool, it can be used for things it wasn't designed for. A hammer is excellent for driving nails and terrible for writing emails. The human brain is excellent for rapid pattern recognition, social navigation, and threat detection in environments with limited information. It is terrible for evaluating statistical evidence, distinguishing correlation from causation, and changing its mind about things it cares about.

Evolution designed us for an environment where quick decisions based on incomplete information were often better than slow decisions based on complete information. The tiger is probably in those bushes. I don't need to verify this. I should run. That logic kept our ancestors alive. Applied to vaccine safety, it suggests that the one story you heard about a child who got sick after vaccination is more persuasive than the epidemiological data from two million children. The brain doesn't know the difference between a tiger and an anecdote.

This chapter is about the specific cognitive shortcuts — the biases — that get exploited by every ridiculous belief in this book. Not because knowing about them will make you immune to them. You won't be. But knowing about them might give you a half-second pause before you share something, which is more than the algorithm gets.

Your Brain Wants to Find Patterns (and It Will, Whether They're There or Not)

The human brain's ability to recognize patterns is extraordinary. It is also totally out of control.

We evolved in an environment where missing a pattern was deadly and finding a false one was mostly harmless. If every time you heard a rustling in the grass something tried to eat you, your brain learned to treat grass-rustling as a danger signal. If you sometimes heard rustling when it was just wind, you ran for nothing — but running for nothing is cheap. Not running when something wanted to kill you was very expensive. So evolution set the sensitivity high. The false positive rate is enormous. We see patterns everywhere.

The QAnon research teams put this on spectacular display. They would take a stream of events — a political resignation, an earthquake, a celebrity's Instagram post, a change in aviation patterns over a city — and find connections. The timing matched. The symbolism aligned. The numbers added up to something significant. None of these connections were real in any causal sense. The brain found them anyway, because the brain that doesn't find patterns gets eaten by the tiger, and the brain that finds too many patterns just occasionally embarrasses itself on the internet.

Ghost hunters take this into architecture. They walk through old buildings with EMF detectors, thermometers, and audio recorders, and find anomalies. The temperature dropped near the door. The audio recording has a sound that, played back at low volume and listened to with intent, sounds vaguely like a word. The EMF detector spiked near the old wiring. These are not supernatural events. They are the normal variability of old buildings with poor insulation, unreliable electrical systems, and acoustic quirks. The pattern-seeking brain presents them as a coherent narrative: there is something here.

Astrology has survived for thousands of years on pattern recognition and nothing else. Believers find the personality traits attributed to their sign reflected in themselves and the people around them. They remember the times the horoscope was accurate. They forget the times it wasn't. The description of Scorpio sounds like them. It also sounds like forty percent of the people they know, because the descriptions are written to be general enough to match a wide range of people — but the brain finds the match and marks it as confirmation.

The flat earthers ran an experiment in this direction that inadvertently illustrated the problem beautifully. In December 2024, a group of believers went to Antarctica to observe the 24-hour sun — a phenomenon that cannot occur on a flat earth model. They saw the 24-hour sun. Several prominent believers acknowledged on camera that their model was wrong. The broader community's response was to declare the expedition fake and accuse their own people of being government plants. The pattern they found in this outcome: the conspiracy is even bigger than we thought.

Your Dramatic Memory Is Lying to You

Here is a simple test. Which kills more Americans per year: sharks or vending machines? The answer is vending machines, by a significant margin — people tip them over trying to get stuck candy and get crushed. Nobody makes summer blockbusters about killer vending machines. Sharks eat one or two people a year in American waters and have terrorized beach attendance since 1975 because a movie made them vivid and memorable. The availability heuristic — your brain's tendency to judge probability by how easily you can recall an example — is not calibrated to reality. It is calibrated to drama.

This is why vaccine fears are more powerful than vaccine benefits, even though vaccine benefits affect millions of children and vaccine injuries affect a statistically tiny fraction. The injury is vivid, specific, and personal: a parent's account of their child changing after a shot, delivered with grief and conviction, directly to your face or your screen. The benefit is statistical: we estimate that vaccines prevent approximately X deaths per year in children under five. Statistics are not vivid. Statistics don't have names. Statistics don't post videos. The one parent's story outweighs the epidemiological data because the epidemiological data cannot compete as a memory.

Alternative cancer treatments seem more effective than they are for the same reason. The people who tried an alternative treatment and died generally don't leave testimonials. They are, in the most direct possible sense, not available for comment. The people who tried an alternative treatment and survived — whether because the treatment worked, because the cancer went into remission naturally, or because they were also doing conventional treatment — are available, vocal, and emotionally compelling. The visible sample is entirely survivors. The dead are invisible. The brain updates on the visible sample.

The manifestation gurus know this and built an industry on it. Every course, every book, every conference is populated by people who visualized something and got it. The millions of people who visualized something, followed the protocols, maintained the gratitude practice, and didn't get it are not featured speakers. They are not on the testimonials page. They are, for the purposes of the evidence you encounter, not real.

If You've Staked Your Identity on It, You Won't Change Your Mind

This is the hardest one to write because it's the most universal. Confirmation bias — the tendency to seek information that supports your existing beliefs and discount information that contradicts them — is not a flaw in certain people. It is a feature of all people. You are doing it right now about something. So am I.

What makes confirmation bias particularly brutal in the contexts we've been exploring is what happens when it combines with identity. If your belief is just an opinion you hold loosely — your preference in restaurants, say — confirmation bias makes you slightly more likely to recommend the place you already like. Low stakes. If your belief is central to who you are, who your community is, what your choices have been, and what you've told other people you stand for, confirmation bias becomes a fortress.

When a parent who publicly opposes vaccines is shown research demonstrating vaccine safety, they don't update toward vaccine safety. They update toward "the research is corrupt." The correction doesn't land on an open mind; it lands on an identity under attack. Accepting the research would mean: the decision they made about their children was wrong. The years of public advocacy were wrong. The community they built their social life around is wrong. The version of themselves as a brave truth-teller fighting a corrupt medical establishment is wrong. That's not an intellectual update. That's a self-dissolution. The brain refuses.

This is why flat earthers at the Antarctic "Final Experiment" in 2024, when confronted with direct evidence that their model was wrong, accused their own expedition members of being compromised. The evidence was too threatening to the identity to process as evidence. It had to be reprocessed as an attack. The more clear and direct the contradiction, the more strongly the belief system defends itself, because the stronger the threat the more the identity needs protection. This is called the backfire effect, and it is the reason that presenting conspiracy theorists with facts often makes them more convinced, not less.

The practical implication is bleak: you cannot reason someone out of a position they didn't reason themselves into. If the belief was adopted for social, emotional, and identity reasons — which most of these beliefs are — then logical arguments are not the right tool. The person isn't in a logical argument. They're defending themselves.

You Believe What Your Tribe Believes

We evolved in small groups where social belonging was not optional. Being expelled from the group meant death — no food, no protection, no reproduction. The social pain of rejection is neurologically real, processed in the same regions of the brain as physical pain, because exclusion from the group was genuinely as dangerous as injury. The pressure to conform to group beliefs is not a weakness or a defect. It is a survival mechanism that is still running, in exactly the wrong context.

When a person's social identity is attached to a belief community — the flat earth movement, the QAnon research community, the anti-vaccine parent group, the manifestation tribe — departing from that belief is not an intellectual exercise. It is a social exile. The people in that community are their friends, their support network, their source of meaning and validation. Questioning the belief means risking all of that. Publicly repudiating the belief means losing all of it.

This is the mechanism that the wellness influencer community runs on with exceptional skill. The community provides emotional support for new parents who feel overwhelmed by conventional medical advice. It provides community, vocabulary, shared values, and a framework that makes you a good and conscious parent rather than a passive consumer of pharmaceutical products. Questioning one part of the belief system — say, the anti-vaccine position — means risking your standing in a community that has become central to your social life. People accept a lot of nonsense to keep their friends.

The other side of tribal thinking is that your tribe's enemies are automatically wrong. Political tribes demonstrate this most visibly. Republicans and

Democrats have switched their stated positions on issues based on which party currently holds them — not over years, but over months, as the tribal cue changed. The position itself is less important than which team holds it. Climate change is the most dramatic example: the scientific evidence has not moved. The tribal affiliations have. The belief follows the team, not the evidence.

Confidence Is Not Competence

The Dunning-Kruger effect has become so widely known that it's almost a cliché, but it's worth meeting it in its natural habitat, which is everywhere you look.

The pattern is this: people with limited knowledge of a field have no way to assess the full scope of what they don't know, so they tend to overestimate their competence. People with extensive knowledge are acutely aware of the field's complexity, the limitations of current understanding, and everything they still don't know — so they express appropriate uncertainty, which reads as weakness to outsiders.

The result is that the anti-vaccine parent who has spent forty hours reading Facebook posts feels more confident about vaccine safety than the immunologist who has spent twenty years studying it. The climate change denier who watched three documentaries feels more confident about climate science than the researcher who has spent a career analyzing ice core data. The confidence gap runs in the wrong direction. The people who know least are most certain; the people who know most are most hedged.

This plays directly into social media dynamics: the confident person is more watchable. The person who says "I've done my research and I know the truth they're hiding from you" is compelling. The person who says "our current best understanding is X, with confidence intervals of Y, subject to ongoing investigation" is less so. The algorithm favors the confident person. The audience favors the confident person. The confident person is often the person who knows least. The system has been optimized to amplify people with the worst epistemic position on any given question.

Andrew Wakefield, who fabricated his data and lost his medical license, spoke to audiences with the absolute confidence of someone who was certain he had discovered something revolutionary. Actual immunologists, discussing the actual evidence, spoke with the appropriate caution of people who understand that science is a process of provisional conclusions updated by evidence. Wakefield sounded like he knew the answer. The immunologists sounded uncertain. The audience, rationally but incorrectly, concluded Wakefield was the credible source.

The Dead Don't Give Testimonials

Survivorship bias is simple: you only hear from the survivors. You don't hear from the people for whom things went badly. This creates a systematic distortion in every testimonial-based field.

Alternative cancer treatments appear to work because the people who tried them and survived are vocal, visible, and emotionally compelling advocates. "I rejected conventional treatment, used this protocol, and I'm cancer-free five years later." This is a real story. What the story doesn't include: the cancer may have gone into remission naturally. The person may have also quietly accepted some conventional treatment. And the people who rejected conventional treatment, used this protocol, and died — they're not in the testimonial database. The dead don't post.

Supplement companies understand this intuitively. The testimonials page features people whose lives were transformed. The people who took the supplement for six months and noticed nothing don't return to fill out the satisfaction survey. The selection process is automatic and unintentional, but it means that the evidence a customer encounters before purchasing is drawn entirely from the population of satisfied customers, which is not the same as the population of all customers.

Manifestation culture runs entirely on survivorship bias. The people featured in manifestation books and courses are people who visualized something and got it. They are the survivors of a much larger group of people who visualized things with equal conviction and didn't get them. The failures are invisible because failure doesn't get invited to speak at conferences, and because the framework itself redefines failure — you failed to manifest because you had limiting beliefs, your vibration was off, you weren't truly aligned. The survivors confirm the theory. The failures are either invisible or absorbed.

Your Brain Hates Losing More Than It Loves Winning

Loss aversion is simple math that the brain gets wrong. Losses feel approximately twice as bad as equivalent gains feel good. Losing twenty dollars hurts more than finding twenty dollars feels good. This is not rational — twenty dollars is twenty dollars — but it's how the psychology works.

In the context of ridiculous beliefs, loss aversion is the glue that keeps people in systems long after the evidence has failed them. The sunk cost of the crystal healing practice, the manifestation coaching program, the two years of anti-vaccine advocacy — admitting those were mistakes doesn't just update a belief. It means acknowledging real losses: time, money, relationships built on those beliefs, and the version of yourself that was certain you'd found the truth. The loss of all that feels catastrophic. Continuing to believe, even in the face of contradictory evidence, feels like preservation. The brain chooses preservation.

The bleach advocates provided the most extreme version of this phenomenon. Parents who had given their children MMS for months, who had watched them experience severe symptoms, who had been told by doctors that their children were being chemically poisoned — some of them continued. The alternative was to accept that they had hurt their children. That loss was too large to process. So the symptoms became detox reactions, the doctors became Big Pharma agents, and the bleach continued.

This is not stupidity. It is a psychological protection mechanism engaging in exactly the situation it evolved for, in a context where it causes catastrophic harm. The brain cannot always tell the difference between a belief that needs protecting and a child that needs protecting. When those two things are in conflict, it sometimes protects the wrong one.

The Biases Are Not Bugs

Every cognitive bias in this chapter was adaptive once. Pattern recognition kept people alive. Loss aversion protected resources. Tribal conformity maintained group cohesion. The availability heuristic produced useful rough estimates in environments where statistical data wasn't available. These aren't failures of the brain. They're features that worked for the environment they evolved for and malfunction in the environment we've built.

The problem is that we now live in an environment saturated with sophisticated agents who know about these biases and design systems to exploit them. Social media companies optimize engagement using the tribal validation mechanism. Supplement companies design testimonial pages to exploit survivorship bias. Conspiracy theory communities provide the social proof and in-group identity that make the tribal conformity bias hold people in place. Alternative medicine practitioners use post hoc reasoning to manufacture the appearance of efficacy.

The biases are running in all of us, all the time, with no off switch and no conscious override. The best available defense is knowing they're there — which makes you marginally better at noticing when you're reaching for one, and maybe gives you a half-second pause before you do. That pause is the whole game. It won't make you rational. Nothing will make you rational. But it might make you slightly less reliably irrational about things that matter, and in the information environment we're currently living in, that's about as much as anyone can ask.

Chapter 18: Conclusion: Why We Believe the Unbelievable

The Human Condition in Digital Age

After touring this museum of human intellectual failure, from flat earthers who think NASA is running the world's most elaborate geography scam to manifestation believers who think the universe operates like a cosmic vending machine, you might wonder how our species ever managed to build civilization in the first place. The answer lies in understanding that the same cognitive mechanisms that make people believe ridiculous things also enabled humanity's greatest achievements.

The pattern recognition that makes conspiracy theorists see hidden connections in random events also helped our ancestors track animals, predict weather patterns, and develop agriculture. The tribal loyalty that turns scientific disagreements into ideological warfare also enabled cooperation on scales that built cities, nations, and global trade networks. The confirmation bias that keeps people trapped in false beliefs also helps maintain social cohesion and individual confidence in uncertain situations.

We're not looking at defective humans who somehow went wrong. We're looking at normal human psychology operating in environments for which it wasn't designed, producing predictable but counterproductive results. Stone Age brains trying to process Space Age information will always produce some spectacular failures alongside genuine successes.

This helps explain why education alone can't solve the problem of ridiculous beliefs. You can't educate people out of cognitive biases any more than you can educate them out of needing food or sleep. These aren't intellectual mistakes that can be corrected through better information; they're systematic features of human psychology that will always influence how we process information, make decisions, and relate to other people.

The Perfect Storm Conditions

The ridiculous beliefs we've explored don't show up randomly. They concentrate in specific conditions, and right now every one of those conditions is running at full intensity simultaneously.

Start with people who are scared, isolated, or feeling like the world is moving without them. That's not a small group in 2026. Economic disruption, institutional decay, the general sense that nobody competent is running anything — these create exactly the psychological environment where false certainty is appealing. When real life feels out of control, a conspiracy theory that explains everything is genuinely comforting, even if the explanation is that lizard people run the Federal Reserve. At least someone's in charge.

Now add the internet, which took every person holding one of these beliefs in isolation and connected them to everyone else who believed the same thing. The flat earther in 1995 was alone. The flat earther in 2026 has a community, a conference schedule, merchandise, and ten thousand people confirming their most important beliefs every time they open their phone. The social friction that previously made it embarrassing to say publicly that you think the moon landing was faked has been removed.

Completely. The algorithm handled the rest — showing the most emotionally provocative version of every claim to the most susceptible audience, repeatedly, with no countervailing information in sight.

Then add money. There is serious money in selling people what they want to believe. The supplement industry, the manifestation coaching industry, the alternative medicine industry, the conspiracy media industry — these are not small operations run by cranks in garages. They are billion-dollar enterprises that have correctly identified a market and are serving it efficiently. The incentive structure rewards whoever tells the most compelling false story with the most conviction. Truth, which is often boring and comes with caveats, cannot compete on engagement metrics.

Finally add the collapse of institutional authority. This is the one that nobody has a good answer to. When people could trust universities, newspapers, government agencies, and professional credentials as rough proxies for reliable information, false beliefs had a harder time getting traction. Those institutions failed repeatedly — some through incompetence, some through corruption, some through arrogance — and the trust they lost didn't go to better institutions. It went to whoever was most confidently telling people what they wanted to hear. Every expert who turned out to be wrong, every institution that lied, every credential that turned out to be for sale, made the next conspiracy theory slightly easier to sell. We did this to ourselves and we're living in the result.

The Ecosystem of Error

The most important insight from our tour of ridiculous beliefs is that they don't exist in isolation but form interconnected systems where different false beliefs support and reinforce each other. Someone who starts by questioning vaccines often encounters flat earth theories, conspiracy beliefs, and alternative medicine claims through the same online communities and information sources.

These belief systems are remarkably resilient because they provide comprehensive explanatory frameworks that can account for any contradictory evidence. When one part of the belief system faces challenges, other parts provide support and rationalization. Flat earthers who can't explain seasons can fall back on claims about government conspiracy. Conspiracy theorists whose predictions fail can decide that disinformation was necessary or that the timeline shifted.

The interconnected nature of false beliefs also means that debunking individual claims often fails because believers can retreat to other parts of their belief system. Proving that vaccines don't cause autism doesn't eliminate anti-vaccine beliefs if people also think that pharmaceutical companies are fundamentally corrupt and that natural immunity is superior. Showing that homeopathy is just water doesn't change minds if people also believe that the medical establishment suppresses natural cures and that water has memory.

This network effect explains why fact-checking and debunking efforts often fail to change minds and sometimes even strengthen false beliefs. When beliefs are part of comprehensive worldviews that provide identity, community, and meaning, individual corrections feel like attacks on the entire system rather than helpful information updates.

The Irony of Intelligence

One of the most disturbing discoveries about ridiculous beliefs is that intelligence doesn't provide immunity against them. In fact, intelligent people are often better at believing ridiculous things because they're more skilled at generating sophisticated justifications for beliefs they want to maintain. Smart people can use their analytical abilities to rationalize predetermined conclusions instead of following evidence to logical outcomes.

This means that education focused on information transmission instead of critical thinking skills can make people more susceptible to certain types of false beliefs. People with advanced degrees can be just as likely to fall for conspiracy theories, alternative medicine claims, or supernatural beliefs as those with less formal education. Intelligence becomes a tool for motivated reasoning instead of truth-seeking.

The conspiracy theory communities we've examined often include engineers, doctors, scientists, and other highly educated professionals who use their technical knowledge to create elaborate alternative explanations for established facts. Their educational backgrounds lend credibility to false beliefs while their analytical skills help them maintain those beliefs against contradictory evidence.

This suggests that protecting against ridiculous beliefs requires more than just access to information or general intelligence. It requires specific skills in evaluating evidence, understanding uncertainty, recognizing cognitive biases, and changing minds when presented with better information. These intellectual virtues aren't automatically produced by education or intelligence but must be deliberately developed.

The Social Cost of Ridiculous Beliefs

While some ridiculous beliefs might seem harmless or even amusing, they impose real costs on people and society. People die when they choose alternative cancer treatments over proven medical interventions. Children suffer when parents reject vaccines based on false fears about autism. Relationships are destroyed when family members fall into conspiracy theory communities that view outsiders as enemies or sheeple.

The social costs extend beyond individual believers to affect entire communities. Vaccine hesitancy threatens herd immunity and puts vulnerable populations at risk. Climate change denial delays necessary policy responses that could prevent catastrophic environmental damage. Election fraud conspiracies undermine democratic institutions and social trust.

Perhaps most importantly, the proliferation of ridiculous beliefs contributes to the breakdown of shared epistemological foundations that make collective problem-solving possible. When people can't agree on basic facts about vaccines, climate change, or election integrity, it becomes impossible to have productive discussions about policy solutions or social coordination.

The time and energy spent on debunking false beliefs, correcting misinformation, and dealing with the consequences of bad decisions based on ridiculous beliefs represents a massive opportunity cost. Instead of working together to solve genuine problems, society must constantly fight intellectual fires started by people who mistake their ignorance for insight.

Digital Age Challenges

The internet age has created unprecedented challenges for maintaining rational belief systems. Information abundance makes it possible to find "evidence" for any position, no matter how ridiculous. Algorithmic content curation creates echo chambers that insulate people from contradictory information. Social media enables rapid spread of misinformation that often travels faster than corrections.

The democratization of information publishing means that anyone can create content that looks professional and authoritative, making it difficult for non-experts to distinguish between reliable and unreliable sources. The collapse of traditional gatekeeping mechanisms removes quality control filters that previously prevented the most obviously false information from reaching large audiences.

Perhaps most challenging is the speed at which false information can spread and establish itself in public consciousness. By the time experts can respond to new conspiracy theories or false health claims, those beliefs may have already reached millions of people and become emotionally embedded in their worldviews. The asymmetry between the speed of misinformation and the speed of correction creates systematic advantages for false beliefs.

These digital age challenges require new approaches to media literacy, critical thinking education, and information system design. Traditional approaches based on expert authority and institutional credibility may be insufficient in environments where all voices seem equally valid and where emotional engagement often trumps factual accuracy.

The Path Forward

People always want to end books like this with a section on what to do about it. I've read those sections in other books. They're full of reasonable suggestions — media literacy education, algorithm reform, rebuilding institutional trust — and they have accomplished approximately nothing, because the problem isn't lack of good ideas. The problem is that the incentive structures running in the opposite direction are enormous and well-funded, and the people who benefit from them are not going to voluntarily stop.

So here's what I actually think instead of what sounds hopeful.

At the individual level, the only thing that reliably works is developing the habit of asking one question before you share anything: does this make me feel good because it's true, or because it confirms something I already believed? That gap — between "this feels true" and "this is true" — is where every ridiculous belief in this book lives. The flat earther isn't lying to you. The MMS parent isn't performing. They genuinely believe what they're telling you. It feels completely true to them. The feeling is the trap, and the only defense is noticing it.

Beyond that: read the primary sources. Not the YouTube video about the study — the actual study. Not the headline — the article. Not the article — the methodology. This is more work and most people won't do it, which is exactly why misinformation spreads through headlines while corrections die in footnotes. If you do it even occasionally, you'll be ahead of most of the people you're arguing with on the internet.

Know when to stop arguing. You cannot reason someone out of a position they didn't reason themselves into. The backfire effect is real — presenting contradictory evidence to someone whose identity is wrapped in a belief often makes them believe harder. What sometimes works is sustained personal relationship, time, and the slow accumulation of trust. What never works is a Facebook argument. Save your energy.

And accept that some percentage of the population is going to believe ridiculous things forever, because that appears to be a stable feature of the species. The goal is harm reduction, not eradication. Vaccines are still worth mandating even if some people will refuse them. Climate policy is still worth pursuing even if some people think it's a hoax. The existence of people who are wrong doesn't mean the right thing stops being right.

The Importance of Intellectual Humility

Perhaps the most important lesson from this look at human intellectual failure is the importance of intellectual humility. Every ridiculous belief we've examined is held by people who are absolutely convinced they're right and that their critics are wrong, ignorant, or malicious. The feeling of being right is identical whether you're right or completely wrong.

This means that confidence is not a reliable indicator of accuracy, and passionate conviction is not evidence of truth. The people who are most certain about their beliefs are often the most likely to be wrong, while genuine experts typically express appropriate uncertainty about the limits of their knowledge.

Intellectual humility involves recognizing the fallibility of human reasoning, the influence of cognitive biases on personal judgment, and the possibility that strongly held beliefs might be incorrect. It means seeking out disagreement rather than confirmation, updating beliefs based on evidence rather than defending predetermined positions, and admitting ignorance rather than pretending to knowledge we don't possess.

This doesn't mean becoming paralyzed by uncertainty or treating all claims as equally valid. It means developing better habits for distinguishing between well-supported and poorly-supported beliefs while maintaining appropriate confidence in our conclusions without becoming overconfident about their certainty.

Why Ridiculous Beliefs Will Always Be With Us

The psychological, social, and technological factors that produce ridiculous beliefs also reveals why they will never be completely eliminated. As long as humans have pattern recognition abilities, we'll occasionally see meaningful connections where none exist. As long as we're social creatures, we'll sometimes adopt beliefs to maintain group membership rather than because they're true. As long as we face uncertainty and mortality, we'll be tempted by beliefs that promise control and meaning.

New technologies will create new opportunities for false beliefs to spread and evolve. New social pressures will create new psychological vulnerabilities that can be exploited by belief entrepreneurs. New scientific discoveries will create new areas of uncertainty where speculation can masquerade as knowledge.

This doesn't mean we should give up trying to promote rational thinking or reduce the social costs of false beliefs. It means approaching these challenges with realistic expectations and sustainable strategies rather than hoping for complete solutions. The goal should be harm reduction rather than perfection, building resilience rather than eliminating all vulnerability.

Final Thoughts: Living with Human Irrationality

After spending considerable time exploring the darkest corners of human reasoning, it's worth remembering that the same species that believes the Earth is flat also sent rockets to the Moon, developed vaccines that save millions of lives, and created technologies that enable global communication and collaboration. Human irrationality coexists with remarkable achievements in science, technology, and social organization.

The challenge isn't to eliminate human irrationality (that's impossible) but to create conditions where our rational capabilities can flourish while minimizing the damage from our inevitable cognitive failures. This requires understanding both our limitations and our strengths, designing institutions that account for human psychology instead of assuming perfect rationality, and developing cultures that reward truth-seeking over confirmation of existing beliefs.

Perhaps most importantly, it requires maintaining compassion for people who believe ridiculous things while still working to reduce the harm those beliefs can cause. The flat earthers, conspiracy theorists, and alternative medicine believers documented in this book aren't evil or fundamentally different from the rest of us. They're normal humans whose cognitive machinery has led them astray in predictable ways that any of us could fall into under the right circumstances.

Knowing why people believe the unbelievable doesn't just help us make fun of their beliefs (though that can be therapeutic). It helps us understand ourselves, recognize our own vulnerabilities to false beliefs, and develop better strategies for navigating an information environment filled with both genuine insight and elaborate nonsense.

The human capacity for believing ridiculous things is the price we pay for the cognitive abilities that make us human. The same pattern recognition, social learning, and abstract thinking that enable science, art, and civilization also make us vulnerable to conspiracy theories, pseudoscience, and supernatural beliefs. Learning to live with this tension, while minimizing its costs, might be one of the most important challenges facing humanity in the digital age.

In the end, the goal isn't to become perfectly rational beings who never fall for false beliefs. The goal is to become slightly better versions of ourselves who are a little more aware of our limitations, a little more careful about our sources, and a little more willing to change our minds when reality disagrees with our expectations. That might not eliminate ridiculous beliefs entirely, but it might help us build a world where truth has a fighting chance against the endless creativity of human self-deception.

What this book comes down to is simple. Every belief in it felt completely reasonable to the people who held it. Every one had community, had "evidence," had an explanation for why critics were wrong. None of that made them right. The measure of a belief is not how good it feels or how many people share it. The measure is whether it survives contact with reality. Most of the beliefs in this

book don't. We can do better than that. We just have to
decide to.

293

About the Author

The author of *Ridiculous Things People Actually Believe* has spent four decades watching humans convince themselves of increasingly creative ways to be spectacularly wrong about basic reality. Unlike the subjects of this book, he knows what he's talking about, making him either an expert or a government agent (depending on which Facebook group you're asking).

For 45+ years in technology leadership, he ran computer operations for Trader Joe's for nearly two decades. That's a $16 billion company where facts correspond to reality or the groceries don't show up. He learned to appreciate the difference between things that work and things people really, really want to work. His technology career began when "doing your own research" meant understanding assembly language, not watching YouTube videos in pajamas.

He's ghostwritten 113+ published books and helped Fortune 50 executives secure $30 million in venture capital and land TEDx speaking opportunities. His books got professionally translated into seven languages. His bestseller "Focus on LinkedIn" sold 15,000 copies in three days. Purdue University uses his book "How to Manage a Consulting Project" as required reading at their business school. Professor Richard Makadok invited him to speak to students multiple times, with sessions consistently rated as the "highlight of the semester."

He's appeared on 55+ podcasts, hosts his own show "Leaders and Their Stories" with nearly 100 episodes, and served as Technical Editor for KnowBe4's cybersecurity book "Cyberheist." He holds multiple CERT emergency response certifications and has a photography portfolio with 950,000+ images. He's survived three earthquakes of 7.1+ magnitude, four hurricanes, and a forest fire. Unlike the people in this book who prepare for imaginary threats, he's dealt with real disasters.

Watching reasonably intelligent humans convince themselves of spectacular nonsense for decades, he decided someone needed to document this phenomenon before it gets completely out of hand. His combination of technical expertise, real-world experience, and fascination with human cognitive failure qualifies him to serve as an anthropologist studying the voluntary intellectual collapse of his own species.

He's spent his career in environments where being wrong has immediate, measurable consequences. This taught him the difference between beliefs that work and beliefs that feel good. In a world full of people absolutely certain about things they're completely wrong about, he offers the perspective of someone who's learned to distinguish between confidence and competence.

You can find more of his work at thewritingking.com.

Books by Richard Lowe

See books by Richard Lowe at
https://masterofworlds.com

Get free publishing insights and industry updates at
https://thewritingking.substack.com

For ghostwriting and book coaching services see
https://thewritingking.com